Until Christ Is Formed in You

Velma Darbo Stevens

Woman's Missionary Union
Birmingham, Alabama

Woman's Missionary Union
P. O. Box 830010
Birmingham, AL 35283-0010

For more information, call 1-800-968-7301 or visit our Web site at www.wmu.com.

Dewey Decimal Classification: 248.843
Subject Headings: CHRISTIAN LIFE—WOMEN
                  SPIRITUAL LIFE
                  BIBLE—STUDY AND TEACHING

Design by Janell E. Young

ISBN: 1-56309-293-X
W994105•0799•5M1

Contents

Introduction

The greatest miracle of Christmas," said the speaker at a Christmastime worship service, "is not God's being incarnate in a human being, Jesus of Nazareth. The greatest miracle is that God is willing to be born in people like you and me."

Then he compared Jesus' body and our bodies to houses. The body of Jesus was a brand-new creation, brought into being by the Holy Spirit—spotless, pure, occupied by God. How different are our bodies! Because very faulty human beings occupy them, they are filled with filth and dirt, with broken windows and sagging doors. The walls are festooned with cobwebs and defiled with graffiti. They are unfit for habitation. Yet God comes to us and offers to make a permanent home in us. What a miracle!

God will not presume to enter our lives without our invitation. Our willingness to turn our lives over to God through Jesus Christ is what we call conversion or the new birth. It signals a profound change in our lives: from living for self to living for God; from walking away from God to walking with God; from being spiritually dead to being spiritually alive—having eternal life.

But this is not all. God does not come to us as a guest, willing to put up with all the deficiencies of our house. God comes not only to live in us but also to change us into a house fit for God's dwelling. What God is after is to turn each of us into a person like the Son of God, Jesus Christ. God wants us to imitate Christ and pattern our lives after His, blessing human beings, bringing the good news of salvation through Christ, caring for God's world, loving God supremely, loving our neighbors as ourselves, and loving other Christians with the self-sacrificing love with which Jesus loved His disciples.

God is not just a guest, gaining access only at our volition. While God will never violate our free will by changing us whether we want to be changed or not, neither will God ever let us alone. God is the Master Builder. God's purpose is to make each person new, according to God's own matchless plan.

It is also part of God's plan to remake all of us who believe in Jesus into what Jesus was like when He lived among human beings. This is not possible in an individual life. No one of us can ever be completely like Jesus. But the "body of Christ," all Christians who exist on this earth, can be like Jesus. They may be in churches, in Bible study classes, in missions groups, in believers banded together for ministry or evangelism or prayer. But they are in essence all one. Their goal is to be like Jesus in this world. It takes all Christians encouraging one another to achieve this goal; but it also takes each person growing as a Christian to "build up" the body of Christ.

This lifelong process is called Christian growth, or spiritual growth. The Holy Spirit living in us is gradually changing us so that we are more like Jesus Christ. All parts of our personalities come under the gentle power of the Spirit of God. The Spirit is never harsh in dealing with us. We are fragile creatures, after all. It is so easy to keep on the path of least resistance, of living like everybody else. But God will never be content until each of us shows more and more clearly what Jesus Christ's life is like in a human being.

This is the reason for the title of this book: *Until Christ Is Formed in You*. It is part of a statement by Paul (Gal. 4:19 NIV): "My dear children, for whom I am again in the pains of childbirth until Christ is formed in you." This is an appropriate quote for women who know, as men never do, what it is like to give birth to a child. (Even if you have never given birth yourself, you know intimately some woman who has.) Paul was not willing to turn his Christian converts loose as long as they needed guidance in becoming like Christ. He knew the long growth process Christians need to become mature in Christ.

Growth cannot occur apart from life. Every higher form of life, both plant and animal, begins with an immature creation; but it carries with it the potential to grow to maturity. Within the organism is everything necessary to bring it to maturity, to the place where it can reproduce itself. Someone once said that a baby is "potential with a push." Anyone who has ever observed a small child trying to push himself up or begin to walk and talk knows what that expression means.

This is also true of spiritual life. We are not born from above fully grown spiritually. But we have potential with a push. We carry within ourselves the power to grow toward spiritual maturity. This is the Holy Spirit. But that potential can be helped or hindered by its environment, whether the conditions for growth are present.

I shall never forget a visit to the meadows above the tree line in the Colorado Rockies. They were filled with flowers that looked remarkably like those in lower elevations: forget-me-nots, lilies, and sunflowers, to name the most familiar. But there were stark differences. Take the sunflowers, for instance. They were true sunflowers, but they stood only four to six inches high. The flowers were larger than the stems that bore them. I learned that it takes four or five years for the alpine flowers to mature so that they will bloom. Every year they grow a little stronger, a little taller. Finally they are mature enough to bloom and produce seed. Then they die.

4

It is amazing that plants will persist in growing to overcome the harsh environment in which they exist. God gives this same power of life to every part of creation. We Christians have that same power in the spirit. But it is up to us to provide the environment in which we can best grow. Alpine flowers must make the best of a difficult situation. We owe it to our God, Who has brought us into the kingdom of love, to provide the best elements for our spiritual growth. There are no magical shortcuts. We need private and public worship, Bible study and the study of Christian books, prayer, fellowship with other Christians, and active service in God's kingdom. Many excellent resources exist to help you grow in these disciplines. The focus of this book is on what spiritual growth involves. But as you read the book, remember that you must provide the environment in which spiritual growth can best take place. Every chapter deals with at least one specific element of spiritual growth. Some chapters may speak to you more clearly than others. You may need to return to some pages later. The hope and prayer with which this book comes to you is that you will continue to grow and mature spiritually "until Christ is formed in you."

1

The Christian's Relationship to God

We begin where spiritual life begins—with our relationship with God. What does it mean to be a Christian? We may be able to describe the process by which a person becomes a Christian, but it is a little harder to define the nature of the relationship with God which comes through trusting belief in Jesus Christ as Savior and Lord of our lives.

Romans 8 is a concentrated statement of what being a Christian involves. This chapter shows how the Christian moves from death to life, from being an outcast to being a child of God, from aimlessness to purpose in living, and from futility to victory.

From Death to Life

Romans 8:1–2,13

"There is therefore now no condemnation" (KJV) is one of the most reassuring statements in the Bible. "Condemnation" means a death sentence. Throughout the first seven chapters of Romans, Paul stressed the fact that the result of living in rebellion against God is death. This is spiritual death, complete separation from God.

Those who rebel against God are separated from God in this life, but not absolutely. God's sun still shines on the just and the unjust. God's seeking love still reaches out to God's estranged children. But this estrangement is the beginning of death.

Christ has delivered His people from this death sentence. Christians have eternal life now. Just as eternal death begins in this world, so does eternal life, for that means relationship with God. This is what it means to be "in Christ": to have a relationship with God through the Son.

This relationship brings not only freedom from death in the hereafter but freedom from sin in the here and now (v. 2). We may not be free from ever sinning, but we are free from the power of sin over us. We see the paralyzing power of sin when we say "I can't" about our lives. We do not recognize our own powers of growth, creativity, love, and greatness. Why do some people fail in courage, in overcoming difficulties, while others in similar circumstances rise to the heights? It is because those in the first group give in to those adverse conditions, while those in the second group rise above them.

Paul explained this principle in verse 13. Readers often misunderstand Paul's terms "flesh" and "Spirit." The "Spirit" obviously means the Holy Spirit, but the "flesh" does not mean our bodies. The Spirit stands for all that is life and power—for godlikeness. The flesh stands for weakness and unlikeness to God.

Paul explained how the Christian could escape from the bonds of living by the flesh. He said that the Christian must "put to death the misdeeds of the body" (NIV). This then is the secret: We get out of the rat race of living by our selfish concerns and our weaknesses as we obey the Spirit. This makes good sense. People who want to break bad habits often make the mistake of concentrating on them. But concentrating on a habit only strengthens it. Finding a different way to react—positively instead of negatively—will weaken the old responses. This is what Paul meant for Christians to do.

This is the basis for spiritual growth. Where there is life, there is growth; and there is no growth without life. We know that we have life because we are "in Christ," and we walk by the Spirit of eternal life.

From Outcast to Child

Romans 8:14–17

Paul did not dwell much on the "from" part of this contrast. He spent most of the first part of his letter dealing with the fact that human beings were out of relationship with God. They were children of God by creation, made in God's image (Gen. 1:26–27). But like the prodigal son they had all chosen to go their own way. They had decided to live in a far country, out of relationship with their Creator and their Father. So, although by creation they could not escape being God's children, by their willfulness they had become estranged from God.

A person who departs totally from her parents' teachings and way of life is still their child by birth. But she is out of relationship with them. By her own will she is an outcast. If she continues on this path throughout her life, she will die an outcast, no longer part of her family. This is a picture of the condition of persons without Christ.

But those who are in Christ have a new relationship with God. Paul gave three criteria by which Christians can know that they are in a genuine relationship with God.

The first evidence is that we Christians "are led by the Spirit of God" (v. 14 NIV). This bears out the fact that it is the relationship with God that counts. When we are living as children of God, we desire above all things to do the will of the Father. We are sensitive to the leading of the Spirit. We may not always do the will of God, and never perfectly. But our wish is to live as God's children, in obedience to God's goodwill for us.

The second evidence is that we have the "Spirit of adoption" (NRSV) rather than the "spirit of slavery." These expressions again remind us of the prodigal son. When he came home, he felt unworthy to have the status of son. He wished to hire out to his father as a servant. To put his feet under the servants' table in his father's house, to work in the familiar fields, to see his father's face—these were his highest ambitions.

But this was not the way his father saw him. This was his beloved son, come back from the dead! His son had been as good as dead because the relationship between them was dead. Now the father was ready to restore his son to the place of honor. He did this symbolically by putting shoes on the son's feet (showing that he did not have to work), a robe on his back (to indicate the dignity of his family), and a signet ring on his finger (to show his authority as one of the master's sons).

Jesus described this new relationship of father and son in terms of the way a Jewish father would have acted. But Paul looked at this situation from the viewpoint of a Roman. He was writing to Roman citizens, and he knew what would appeal to them: the status of adopted son.

In the Roman family the father's will was supreme. His minor children had no more status than his slaves did (see Gal. 4:1–2). The father could mistreat his sons, disinherit them, even have them killed, and no law would touch him. But if he should adopt a child, the situation was different. Roman law protected the adopted child's status. If the law said that this was the father's son, he could not be disinherited or disowned. No matter what he might do, or what problems might arise between him and his adoptive father, his place as a son was secure.

Paul used this powerful figure to impress on his readers their security as children of God. They had been children of God through creation. Now they were children of God through God's deliberate choice and will: They were adopted!

Christians need not feel enslaved or fear God. Instead, they can boldly call God, Abba, Father. This beautiful word *Abba* is largely lost on us because we do not understand Aramaic, which Jesus spoke. Abba was the familiar name for one's father. It would be like our Daddy or Papa. It was the first name that a little child used in addressing her father. It speaks of warm affection, of closeness and intimacy. It is the word Jesus used when addressing His Father in heaven (see Mark 14:36). This tells us how close we can come to our God—not a Creator Who is far away in the heavens, but a loving Parent with Whom we can be on intimate terms.

The third evidence Paul gave was internal—heart to heart. He said, "God's Spirit makes us sure that we are his children." Notice two things in this statement.

Verse 16 in the Greek uses a different word for "children" than in verse 14. There the word translated "children" is *sons* in the Greek. In verse 16 the word for "children" means a child by birth. *Sons* speaks of the formal relationship—having the status of an heir. *Children* speaks of the personal relationship, the warm feeling of closeness between parent and child.

Also notice that Paul stressed the inward character of this witness. When all outward signs and assurances fail, the word God speaks within our hearts is the best. When we hear an inner assurance that we belong to God as children, we can believe that assurance. It comes from God through the Holy Spirit.

So all of us who have wandered in the far country of selfishness and have come home can revel in the thought that we are God's beloved children. We are children of God just as Christ is God's child (see v. 29). God loves us just as much as that only begotten Son. More, God shows surpassing love through giving Christ up for all human beings (v. 32). With this relationship we have a secure base from which to grow and a great ideal toward which to grow—our Elder Brother (v. 29).

From Aimlessness to Purpose

Romans 8:13,17–18; 2 Corinthians 4:6; 3:18

The word *aimlessness* can mean having no purpose at all. But it can also refer to the kind of fluctuating purpose one never achieves. Or, if the person meets the goal, she finds it to be unsatisfactory. Then the person begins to search for another goal.

I remember a couple whom my parents knew when I was a child. They had a beautiful nineteenth-century home on a spacious boulevard. Their passion was enhancing the woodwork in their home. They invited us to see their accomplishments. With deep pride they exhibited the new mantel, the new banisters, even new veneer on dining table and chest of drawers. Every piece of wood had been covered or embellished in some way. They had only a few pieces left to finish when we visited them.

About a month later my father was astounded to see an ad in the newspaper offering this beautiful home for sale. He called his friend, not believing what he had seen. The friend answered that they had grown tired of the project. They were now pursuing their dream of owning a farm in the country!

A vital purpose in living is important for everyone. And the Christian, whether she recognizes it or not, already has a supreme purpose. It is "to glorify God and enjoy God forever."

What does it mean to "glorify God"? There are a lot of possible meanings, but perhaps it is best to get back to the original meaning of the word *glory* as related to God. Exodus 33:12–23; 34:4–7,29 give the account of the way Moses experienced God's glory. "Glory" in these verses was the splendor of God so far as human beings could comprehend it. This glory, God said, was so excruciatingly bright that no one could behold it and live. It might be compared to looking full into the sun—and being struck blind.

Paul commented on this Old Testament experience in 2 Corinthians 3–4. Two verses in these chapters shed light on our purpose in glorifying God. Paul said in 2 Corinthians 4:6 that we have "the light of the knowledge of the glory of God in the face of Christ" (NIV). In other words, Jesus shows us what God is like—God's glory. Someone has said, "If God had a face, it would be the face of Jesus Christ."

In 2 Corinthians 3:18 (NRSV) Paul made it clear that we, too, are the faces of God. "All of us, with unveiled faces, seeing the glory of the Lord as though reflected in a mirror, are being transformed into the same image from one degree of glory to another." We move from one degree of glory—of showing God to the world—to ever higher degrees as we grow into the likeness of Jesus Christ. So, to glorify God is to show the rest of humankind Who God is.

This is the purpose of the Christian as she grows toward "the likeness of [God's] Son" (Rom. 8:29 NIV). Our glorifying of God becomes our own glorification (2 Cor. 4:17). Like a little girl who harbors an ambition to be "just like my mommy," glorifying God—becoming like God—is the prospect in front of us, and this is the purpose of our living.

How do we carry out this purpose? Paul made it clear that being glorified involves suffering (Rom. 8:17). What kind of suffering? Do we seek out trouble or inflict pain on ourselves? Not at all. We suffer with Christ. This means we suffer as He did and for the same reasons.

Jesus lived His whole life in the context of doing the will of God. Carrying out this purpose brought Him continually into conflict with the different standards and expectations of people around Him. The resulting tensions caused Him suffering.

12

It is the same for Jesus' disciples. In following the leading of the Spirit, we come into conflict with the world. The tension causes suffering. But Paul assured his readers that the suffering they would undergo in this life would be as nothing compared to the glory they would have at the end of time (Rom. 8:18). This assurance is a great part of the Christian's victory.

From Futility to Victory

Romans 8:18,35–39

The end of a life lived in rebellion against God is death (Rom. 8:13). This is the ultimate in futility: to put in a whole lifetime with nothing to show for it in the end.

But the end of earthly life for the Christian is the glory that is her inheritance from God (Rom. 8:17–18). This is the ultimate in victory. What about the meantime? Do we have to wait till the end of time to gain the victory God has promised?

By no means! The end of chapter 8 is a shout of victory. God has already won the victory over all the forces of evil. We share now in that victory (see Rom. 8:37). It comes to us in the form of God's love in Christ Jesus. God's love is unconquerable. At the end of Romans 8, Paul piled up all kinds of catastrophes and troubles that might befall the followers of Christ. He spoke of the persecutions that might well be the lot of those who suffered with Christ. Paul himself had gone through many of these trials. He declared that in these experiences Christians are more than conquerors.

Paul went on to rack his brain for other disasters which might strike fear in people's hearts: death, unseen spiritual powers, the unknown future. At last, as if in desperation, he threw in "anything else in all creation." He seemed to want to be sure that he had included the entire created universe. Nothing in that universe, which includes everything except the uncreated One, the very God, will be able to separate God's children from God's love.

This is the ultimate victory—not the victory we will have at the end of time, but the victory we can know right now. If we are secure in God's love, who or what can defeat us? "If God is for us, who can be against us?" (Rom. 8:31 NIV).

Questions for Thought and Discussion

(Use these questions individually or in a small-group discussion. They are not designed to elicit factual or right and wrong answers. Their intent is to probe each woman's heart and spirit. Christian growth is individual. The more deeply a woman examines her own life, the more true will be her response to God's call for spiritual growth.)

1. When you think of God, what names or terms come to your mind? How do they make you feel? Glad? Fearful? Humble? Uncertain?

2. How would you describe your relationship to God? Just beginning? Growing? Dynamic? Confusing? Leveled off? Stagnant? Rewarding?

3. Look again at the different ways this chapter explains how being related to God changes a person. Which of these "From ___ to ____" headings describe your present spiritual growth? Which ones do you wish you could claim, but you do not yet feel comfortable about?

Personal Action Plans

Recognizing that my personal relationship with Christ has brought me from death to life, I will allow God to unleash God's powers of growth, creativity, love, and greatness in me and will work to

Believing my personal relationship with Christ seals my adoption as God's daughter, I will demonstrate my kinship to God by

I determine to show the world what God is like by

Declaring that my personal relationship with Christ gives me victory in all things, I give to God my feelings of futility and fear about _____________ and thank God for this victory.

2

Growing in Self-Worth and Integrity

This and the following two chapters will focus on the basic elements of Christian growth which contribute to our growing in likeness to Christ: self-worth and integrity, faith and wisdom, power and persistence.

As you think of self-worth, you may be asking, "Why is this one of the qualities basic to Christian growth? I would think that self-denial would be more important."

I got my best insight into what self-worth means in a study of John 13:1–5. I had read this passage many times. The thing that always stood out for me was Jesus' act of humility. But once when I was reading it, a different portion of the text suddenly hit me in the face: "Jesus knew . . . that he had come from God and was returning to God" (NIV). In a flash these words put new meaning into Jesus' act of washing His disciples' feet. When He took the part of a servant, He was not forgetting Who He was! In fact, the very security of that knowledge made it easier for Him to do the distasteful but necessary job of washing the dirt and grime from the feet of the company.

This is what self-worth involves. It means realizing our worth and importance in the sight of God. It is a clear recognition of who we are: persons made in the image of God and redeemed by the death of God's Son.

Integrity becomes a natural outgrowth of this kind of self-awareness. Another word for integrity is *integration*. This is the binding together of all parts of a person—physical, mental, emotional, spiritual—so that the parts are working together for the good of the whole person.

The words *integrity* and *integration* are both related to a Latin word *integer*, meaning whole or entire. The person who knows herself to be God's child will not allow parts of herself to be hidden from her awareness. She will want to bring all these parts into consciousness and to be sure that they are available for God to use in service.

Integrity grows naturally from integration of life. A person with integrity acts toward others out of her own wholeness. She does not behave one way to some people and another way to others. She does not lie or cheat. She does not satisfy one part of her being at the expense of the whole, such as indulgence in food or drink at the expense of her body.

Persons with self-worth and integrity have basic equipment for spiritual growth. Look at some Bible passages that expand on these qualities.

The True Humanity

Galatians 3:26–28

Differences among people are so much a part of our human existence that they seem natural. Differences exist in every age and every culture. Something in human nature seems to insist on a pecking order, a system of higher and lower. People look for ways to put one another down.

In the first century devout Jewish men prayed a prayer of thankfulness for their "differences." Each morning a Jewish man would pray, "God, I thank Thee that Thou hast not made me a Gentile, a slave, or a woman."

Paul came from a devout Jewish family. Quite probably he had heard this prayer and even prayed it himself. It may have been in his mind when he wrote Galatians 3:28, in which he declared that the differences so cherished among people on an earthly plane have no validity in the kingdom of God.

Paul first stated a favorite theme: "In Christ Jesus you are all children of God" (Gal. 3:26 NRSV). Those who are all in one family do not emphasize their differences. They consider the ties that bind them together much more important.

In Galatians 3:28 Paul made his great "emancipation proclamation." He stated firmly that all the differences people set up have no effect in the family of God. Here there is no longer Jew or Greek (differences based on religious background), slave or free (economic and social differences). Even the natural biological differences between male and female are no longer important. In the Greek the word for "or" separates the first two pairs. But Paul wrote, "There is no longer male *and* female" (NRSV). He recognized the basic differences that exist between the sexes, but membership in the family of God transcends these. Those who criticize Paul for being "antiwomen" might well ponder this verse.

Why are these differences not important in the family of God? Because "you are all one in Christ Jesus" (NIV). Several years ago someone coined the phrase *the new humanity* for Christians. It might be even more accurate to speak of *the true humanity*. This is what God intended from the beginning. God desires all humanity, made in the divine image, to grow in bearing that image.

I am glad that Paul included the very real differences of gender along with the other differences such as religious, social, and economic status. Those who are one in Christ Jesus rise above even the most basic biological differences. This implies that other conditions at birth, such as variations in mental and physical ability, do not matter in the kingdom of God. It is true, as one person has said, that "the ground is level at the foot of the Cross."

This sense of self-worth makes it both possible and necessary to treat all other people as equal in importance. We cannot discount another person's humanity just because she or he is not like us in some respect. Integrity means treating everyone with respect, with the consideration that we desire for ourselves.

The Children of God

1 John 3:1–3

In this beautiful passage John repeated the emphasis Paul so often reinforced—that we are the children of God. But John added some special touches of his own. The word he used for children *(tekna)* is the same word Paul used in Romans 8:16. It means the special birth relationship between parents and child. John also made it plain that such a relationship was not just in words, but in actuality.

John rhapsodized over the love bestowed on us by the Father. J. B. Phillips catches the spirit of John's words: "Consider the incredible love that the Father has shown us in allowing us to be called 'children of God'—and that is not just what we are called, but what we are."

John also explained the hostility of the world toward Christians: If we are children of God, even as Jesus is the Son of God, we cannot expect better treatment than He received. He was in the world as a king in disguise, so to speak. In legend kings sometimes disguised themselves so that they could move among their people and find out their needs and concerns. Sometimes these kings were mistreated because others did not recognize them. Similarly, many people did not recognize Jesus as the Son of God, and they mistreated Him.

John put a future dimension into the idea of being children of God. He reminded his readers of the end result of their relationship with God—to be like their Elder Brother. "When he appears" (NIV) in His glory, to our joy we will find ourselves like Him. When we are confronted with His reality, all our imperfections will be swept away. We will not lose our own personalities. But we will reflect God's glory even as Jesus reflects God's glory (see Jesus' prayer in John 17:20–24).

What a basis for self-worth 1 John 3:1–2 reveals! We can be as closely related to God the Creator as a child is to her deeply loving parent! And we can become as much like that Parent—that wonderful heavenly Parent—as a redeemed human being can be! Anyone who has such a relationship with God and such a hope for eternity cannot be defeated by the world. She cannot be put down by her own sense of inadequacy.

John went on to speak very plainly of what we are calling integrity. In verse 3 he stated that every person who has the hope of bearing Christ's likeness in heaven "purifies" herself. This purification goes on continually in this life.

The Beatitudes record the account of Jesus blessing those who are "pure in heart, for they will see God" (NIV). We can compare purity there and in this verse to the use of the word *pure* in food products. Pure honey, for instance, guarantees that the honey is unadulterated, unmixed with other ingredients. Apply this meaning to 1 John 3:3 and Matthew 5:8. Jesus was Who He was, an integrated personality, fully devoted to doing the will of His Father. Only those whose inner being is totally devoted to knowing God will see God.

Integrity, then, consists of also devoting oneself more and more to being what one is—a child of God. As adulterations are strained away and sinful motives purged, we become more and more like the Son of God. Thus we are getting ourselves ready for the day when "we shall be like him" (NIV) in completeness.

The One Body—Many Gifts

1 Corinthians 12:4–7,12

It is probably fortunate for Christians of all the centuries that the early churches had so many problems. Paul in particular wrote a number of letters to settle problems in these churches. Some of these letters have come down to us with wisdom we can apply to our own lives.

The Corinthian church had an abundance of problems. Perhaps one reason was that they were an active, thriving church. One of their problems had to do with spiritual gifts. Church members displayed so many gifts that they disputed the relative importance of specific ones.

Relevant points for us as we think about self-worth are that (1) all Christians have spiritual gifts; (2) these gifts come from the Spirit of God; and (3) God gives them for the good of the whole church.

Paul coupled the ideas of varied gifts and one Giver in verses 4–6. The Bible in Today's English Version provides a very clear reading of this passage: "There are different kinds of spiritual gifts, but the same Spirit gives them. There are different ways of serving, but the same Lord is served. There are different abilities to perform service, but the same God gives ability to everyone for their particular service." We can see from this reading that no matter what the gift, God gives it for the purpose of service.

Verse 7 further underlines this point: "To each is given the manifestation of the Spirit for the common good" (NRSV). Spiritual gifts come to each Christian, not for the person to enjoy for herself but "for the common good." And what is the common good? It is the good of the church, the body of Christ (v. 12). It is astounding to read Paul's words, "So it is with Christ." The church is not *like* Christ's body. It *is* Christ's body.

Like a physical body, the church is one, though made up of various members with different functions. But the gifts of all these members exist for the good of the whole body, of Christ Himself.

At this point it is important to define the church as the body of Christ. All the Christians living in the world constitute the body of Christ on earth. Every person has an effect on the world around her and also an effect, through the power of the Holy Spirit, upon the whole world. She may do this through prayer, through giving to bring the good news to persons far beyond her ability to reach, through living in such a way that her "good deeds" go far beyond her.

At the same time, each group of Christians, large or small, also constitutes the body of Christ. Paul was speaking of the church in this latter sense in 1 Corinthians 12. It is in the local body of Christians that we exercise our gifts for the common good. We coexist in vital relationship with one another. Our gifts, like the parts of a healthy body, enhance the body's life. Take the eye. It does not pause to revel in its ability to perceive color, detail, and movement. Immediately it sends its signals to the brain, so that the whole body may profit by what the eye sees.

What do these verses tell us about self-worth and integrity? First, every Christian has spiritual gifts. There is no part of the body without a function (except perhaps the appendix!). If a person is a part of the body of Christ, she has a gift from the Spirit for her to use. These gifts are not to be rated as more or less important. They are all necessary to the proper working of the body. Every person in the church can have a sense of worth because each contributes to the working of the body.

Second, integrity means using one's gifts for the common good. Sometimes church members refuse to use their gifts because they feel theirs are not important or because they do not want to be bothered. When this happens, just that much of the body of Christ is diminished. A Christian working out of her integrity will use her gift for the good of the church and for the glory of Jesus Christ.

The Community of God's People

1 Peter 2:5,9–10

The church is the body of Christ. But the church is also a community with a high and holy calling. Peter described the community of Christians in the most exalted terms, many of which come from Old Testament passages.

Verse 5 refers to the "living stones" (NIV). In Peter's view the Christian community was being fitted together to form a dwelling for God, "a spiritual house." Peter was comparing the whole church to the Temple at Jerusalem. Some important things to remember about these living stones: Each is necessary for the building of the house; each must fit with the others. If each person is not included, or if individuals cannot fit with each other, the house will have great gaps, or the structure will not fit together harmoniously in places.

Christians are not only to form God's house but also to offer the sacrifices that are necessary to worship in the Temple. Peter did not define these sacrifices beyond saying that they were spiritual, not material. His words remind us of Romans 12:1, where Paul called for Christians to give themselves to God as living sacrifices.

In verse 9 Peter piled one image on top of another as he tried to make clear to his readers the privileges of the people of God. First, they are "a chosen people." Israel had prided itself on being the Chosen People. Now the "chosen people" are those who have a relationship with God through their trusting submission to Jesus as Lord.

Christians, Peter said, are also "a royal priesthood." This phrase probably means a group of priests attached to the king, as we would speak of the royal guardsmen. The priests are not only holy, fit to offer sacrifices (v. 5), but are also specifically set aside by the King of kings.

The Christian community is also "a holy nation." God set Israel apart to be "a holy nation" (Ex. 19:6). God chose them and ruled them. Now, Peter said, Christians are citizens of just such a nation.

Perhaps the most beautiful picture Peter drew is one translated "God's own people." The marginal note in the *New Revised Standard Version* indicates that the literal sense of the Greek words is "a people for his possession." "Possession" in the Greek means something undertaken or achieved for one's own self. It might be used of money belonging to a woman that did not come from her husband. It was her "special possession." Peter actually quotes this phrase from Exodus 19:5 (NIV), which says, "You will be my treasured possession." This expression in the Hebrew meant the treasure of a king that he reserved especially for himself, apart from the royal treasury. So the Christian community is God's "treasured possession," a special wealth belonging to God alone.

Are these great attributes purely for the sake of God's people? Are we to take pride in being God's chosen people? Certainly not!

Peter immediately stated the purpose for which the people of God are set aside. They are to proclaim to a lost world the great deeds of the One Who has called them "out of darkness into his wonderful light" (NIV). This is the witnessing mission of the church. It is the job of Christians to carry into all the places where they live and work the good news of what God has done for them in Christ Jesus.

What is this good news? That we who once were "not a people" are now "God's people." That we who once "had not received mercy . . . now . . . have received mercy" (NIV). Peter quoted this from Hosea 2:23. The

24

prophet Hosea had predicted to his sinful fellow citizens that they would eventually repent and that God would hear and restore them. So it still is for every person who turns from sin and self, throwing herself or himself upon the mercy of God. This is our motivation for witnessing—our love for our neighbors and our hope that they too may come to experience the mercy of God, even as we have.

What a glorious identification for the Christian! To be a living stone in God's temple, a priest who serves the King, a member of God's chosen people, a citizen of a holy nation, and a part of God's prized possession. How could anyone deny her own worth in the face of such assurances?

Out of this sense of worth comes the greatest motivation for integrity. We are not part of the community of God in order to claim our privileges and clutch them jealously to ourselves. In integrity we make our deeds match our sense of who we are. Because we know that God loves us so much, we are able to love God with all of our mind and soul and heart and strength. That love motivates us to extend God's offer of reconciliation to every other person. As we are faithful to our calling, others will become part of the community of God's people.

Questions for Thought and Discussion

1. How do you feel about yourself? Do you wish you were different? Do you feel comfortable with who you are? (You may wish to compare your findings with another woman in your study group or with a close Christian friend.)

2. Describe integrity. How does it relate to integration of life?

3. How does seeing yourself as a child of God increase your sense of self-worth? Notice the descriptions of the people of God in 1 Peter. Apply each of these to yourself (and to others in your group) and see how they change your sense of self-worth.

4. How can you use the gifts God gives you for the common good? What effect does your integrity have on the way you use your gifts?

Personal Action Plans

Recognizing that membership in the family of God transcends all differences that exist among people, I will begin or further develop a relationship with

Believing that I am a child of God in a family where there are many children, I will work at becoming more and more like the Son of God by

Affirming that God's Spirit has given me spiritual gifts for the good of the whole church, I will further develop and use my spiritual gift(s) of _______________ by

Declaring that God's love motivates me to extend God's offer of reconciliation to others, I will share this love and offer with _______________ this week by

3

Growing in Faith and Wisdom

Faith and wisdom form the second couplet in the elements of Christian growth.

What does it mean to have faith? We often define faith as an affirmation of theological truths. For instance, we may say, "I believe in the Atonement of Jesus." We may even be able to tell what we think the Atonement means. But that statement, by itself, falls far short of faith. Faith is the willingness to stake your whole life on a truth in which you believe. For example, you may say, "I believe that airplane will fly." But unless you get on the airplane and allow it to carry you into the sky, you don't truly have faith. So it is with belief in the Atonement of Jesus. As long as our belief is only of the head, the Atonement does not benefit us. Staking our whole life on what Jesus has done in His atonement is faith.

Wisdom deals with mental processes. The wisdom of which the Bible speaks is the ability to observe truth and choose to live according to it. Wisdom is far more than knowledge. Knowing facts can help a person pass a test or get a job. But the ability to put those facts to work is wisdom. Knowledge may get you through school, but wisdom gets you through life!

What Is Faith?

Hebrews 11:1–6

The word *faith* occurs over and over in the Bible. We talk a lot about faith, but what does it really mean? This passage from Hebrews provides one of the best definitions of faith in all of the Bible.

The first verse begins with the significant word *now.* This word is a signpost. It points back to something the writer has already said. Look at Hebrews 10:39 (NRSV): "But we are not among those who shrink back and so are lost, but among those who have faith and so are saved." The writer of Hebrews had been discussing the need for persistence in the Christian life. He finished what he was saying by declaring that those who had faith would endure. In the next sentence he defined what he meant by faith.

All of the words in this verse are important. The Greek word for assurance is *hypostasis.* In English it refers to a substance, a basis, or a support. This is what assurance means with reference to faith. Faith gives substance to what God has promised for the future.

Consider the way people use the word translated "conviction" in criminal court trials. A person may be convicted only on sufficient evidence. The justice system will not allow hearsay, bias, rumors, or abstract reasoning. Convictions should result only from solid evidence beyond a reasonable doubt.

The writer of Hebrews declared that what people cannot grasp with their senses, they can grasp through the faculty of faith. While these realities may not be visible, they are nonetheless real. Faith, then, becomes a kind of sixth sense for the Christian. By faith Christians have convincing evidence of the unseen spiritual world.

Jesus gave a good illustration of the faculty of faith in His parable of the mustard seed. Though it is almost infinitesimal, Jesus said, the seed contains within itself the power to become one of the tallest and broadest plants in the garden. So, when a person of faith holds a tiny seed in her hand, she does not feel only the bare touch of the tiny seed. She does not see it almost lost in the lines of her palm. Instead, she sees the tall plant spreading its branches afar. She recognizes the power that lies in the tiny seed, the very power of life itself.

This parable illustrates the definition of faith: Faith gives assurance to the promises of God in which we hope. And faith provides conviction of the unseen spiritual world of which we are citizens and heirs.

The writer of Hebrews gave an outstanding example of the way faith works to provide evidence (v. 3). No material exists to prove that God created the world. But through the faculty of faith we "understand that the worlds were prepared by the word of God" (NRSV).

In the remainder of Hebrews 11, the writer illustrated the working of faith as giving substance to God's promises. Two heroes of the faith are Abel and Enoch. Abel's death was the first recorded in the Bible. He died well before his time, the victim of his brother's murderous hate. Enoch, on the other hand, did not die at all. He was "taken so that he did not experience death" (NRSV). Both pleased God in their lives. Both operated by faith in God's promises. And both considered spiritual realities to be more important than the material world.

The writer of Hebrews made a summary statement in verse 6 that is in a way another definition of faith. Faith consists in believing that God exists and that God will reward those who seek Him by a self-revelation to them. Both parts of this statement of faith are important. Many people throughout the world believe in a supreme being. Many believe in God. But they do not necessarily believe that God makes a revelation to individuals or that God rewards their search.

God is trustworthy. Faith holds to that as much as it holds to the fact that God exists. "If we are faithless, he remains faithful—for he cannot deny himself" (2 Tim. 2:13 NRSV). God is the one constant in the completely inconstant world in which we live.

What Is Wisdom?

1 Corinthians 2:11–16

Wisdom is one of the great words of the Bible. Biblical writers use the word *wisdom* to indicate the understanding of spiritual truth. Such understanding leads to strong spiritual lives, free from harm, creative, and fulfilling. (Read Prov. 3:21–26.)

This passage in 1 Corinthians defines wisdom as "spiritual intelligence." Paul compared this kind of intelligence with human wisdom and showed how it excelled.

It takes a human being to understand the thoughts of another human being (v. 11). A dog or a cat may live all the time with a person and "seem" like a person itself. But it cannot understand all that its owner says to it. Certainly there cannot be human communication between the two. Just so, Paul said, only a spiritual being—the Spirit of God—can understand the thoughts of God. Christians have received the Holy Spirit in order to understand God's communication.

God's Spirit provides spiritual wisdom (v. 13), which we need in order to compare spiritual things with spiritual. This can involve several ideas. It may mean matching spiritual persons to spiritual truths; matching spiritual ideas to spiritual words; interpreting spiritual ideas to spiritual persons; or combining spiritual ideas with spiritual words. Fortunately, we do not have to choose among these possibilities. All of them are true. Only spiritual persons can understand spiritual truths.

Spiritual ideas must be conveyed in spiritual terms. The total idea is that spiritual wisdom deals in a realm that is outside the scope of merely human knowledge.

Paul underlined this fact in verse 14 when he said that spiritual truths seem like "foolishness" to the "unspiritual" person. Such a person uses only reason or logic to grasp truths. She will find the truths imparted by God to be "foolishness." They will make no sense to her.

On the other hand, the spiritual person is qualified to sift, examine, and judge all things. This person has the wisdom to discern truth and separate it from falsehood. Her superior judgment puts her above the judgment of "unspiritual" people. They cannot understand her or explain her. While her decisions make sense to her, they may not make sense to anyone else.

In fact, Christians may often find themselves feeling isolated or disconnected from the mainstream of society because of the choices and decisions their spiritual wisdom encourages them to make. A Christian may experience ridicule, misunderstanding, misjudgment, and other less-than-positive reactions from those outside the Christian family. A Christian's lifestyle, decisions, and choices are not always "reasonable" and "logical," especially when they are Christlike. Jesus experienced such misunderstanding regularly, even among His close followers. Always the patient Teacher, Jesus lovingly and consistently lived the lessons He taught, proving the value and excellence of spiritual wisdom.

What is the essence of this wisdom? Paul summed it up in one short phrase: "the mind of Christ." In the Greek the word translated "mind" means intelligence or consciousness. So, to have the mind of Christ means to be endowed with His capacity for understanding spiritual truths, for comprehending the thoughts of God. Jesus had the Spirit in full measure. We have that same Spirit. It is what makes us spiritual persons. This is the meaning of wisdom: spiritual intelligence, such as Jesus Christ possessed.

What Does Faith Bring?

James 1:5–8

Where does wisdom come from? James declared that it is the gift of God, bestowed in answer to the prayer of faith.

Christians receive both faith and wisdom from God in the experience of conversion. What, then, did James mean? Look at the preceding verses. James had been discussing the problems of trials for the Christian. He moved almost abruptly to the subject of wisdom. Perhaps he meant that Christians, in the face of trials, need to pray for wisdom to face their difficulties. Compare this situation to the difference between native intelligence and using that intelligence to the full. All Christians have wisdom, but not all use it to the full. The capacity to use wisdom in specific circumstances, as well as the gift of wisdom, comes from God. It comes as Christians pray for it.

James placed a lot of emphasis on the need for praying in faith, "never doubting." This is a graphic word in the Greek. It literally means "tossed back and forth." Luke used the word in Luke 8:24 to describe storm-tossed waves. If you have ever been on or near a body of water during a storm, you know how unstable the water is. It dashes and tosses like a wild thing. This was the way James described a person who tries to pray without a steady faith in God. James called such a person "double-minded and unstable in every way" (NRSV).

Why will the "unstable" person not receive an answer to her prayers? Recall the definition of faith: Believing that God exists and through our faithful responses to God we receive answers to our prayers. Faith gives assurance of the future and conviction that the spiritual world exists. So a person who prays without faith cannot receive an answer. She will not really believe that God will answer her prayer. Nor will she be capable of seeing beyond the material world to the spiritual. She continues to struggle on, tossed back and forth, first believing that God will help her and then refusing to believe.

This does not mean that a person must have "enough" faith in order to pray for wisdom. The contrast is not between "much" faith and no faith. It is the contrast between having even a "grain of mustard seed" of faith and the doubt that accompanies refusal to believe in God's promises.

What Does Wisdom Bring?

Ephesians 1:17–20

We have seen that faith brings wisdom. What does wisdom bring to spiritual growth? Is it just a heightened common sense? Not according to Paul! In this portion of one of his great prayers, he clearly stated the content of wisdom. This content is of the greatest value in spiritual growth.

Paul addressed his prayer to "the God of our Lord Jesus Christ." The God Who bestows the gift of wisdom is the One revealed by Jesus Christ. God is also "the Father of glory." This may mean the source of glory or the one who is preeminently glorious. Either meaning fits.

Paul's first petition was that the Ephesians might receive a "spirit of wisdom and revelation" (NRSV). There is no article with "spirit" in the Greek. Paul therefore was likely not referring to the Holy Spirit. He probably meant an inner spirit of teachableness. This would grow as they came "to know him," that is, God.

Then Paul prayed that the "eyes" of their hearts would be "enlightened." This idea goes back to the way faith works. It "sees" what is invisible. Paul wanted his readers to have a clear vision of God's revealed truth. What is that truth? It encompasses past, present, and future. The more of it we understand, the greater will be our ability to grow in spiritual life and power.

Look to the *past,* to "the hope to which he has called you." Paul was always referring to God's purpose from the foundation of the world (see Eph. 1:4–6), which was to save God's people and glorify them. The first phase of wisdom then is to recognize God's calling, to accept it, and to live it out. We can embrace this calling in full confidence. It is no new thing with God, hastily conceived. Even before creation it was part of God's purpose for us and for all humankind throughout the ages!

Look to the *future:* "the riches of his glorious inheritance among the saints." We generally think of ourselves as having an inheritance from God. Here Paul stressed the fact that God's children are God's own inheritance. It is what God is working on as a legacy to the whole universe for all eternity. God will display these glorified children as the result of what God has done in and through them. We will bear God's glory in ourselves, and this will be God's glory.

This phase of wisdom provides impetus for spiritual growth. (Recall 1 John 3:1–3.) Our lives are like weaving a tapestry or creating a crewel embroidery picture—every added thread builds up the picture and increases its beauty.

Look to the *present* (v. 19). It is almost impossible to translate this verse. Paul piled up words to express the overwhelming power God makes available to God's people. Paul used three separate words for power. With it he used the word translated "exceeding." This word comes from a Greek verb meaning "to throw across or

34

beyond," so it is "over and above." Compare Paul's statement in Ephesians 3:20.

You can see how difficult it is to get all these ideas into English! The *Revised English Bible* has one of the best renderings: "How vast are the resources of his power open to us who have faith. His mighty strength was seen at work when he raised Christ from the dead."

All this power is available to us every day! This phase of wisdom points us to our never-failing source of power for living.

Faith + Wisdom = Spiritual Growth

Faith believes not only that God exists but also that God has a rewarding relationship with God's children.

Faith gives substance to the future. It enables us to "see the unseeable," the spiritual world.

The prayer of faith brings wisdom.

Wisdom is spiritual intelligence, "the mind of Christ," given so that we may comprehend spiritual truths.

These spiritual truths are the thoughts of God toward humanity. They tell us that God planned from the beginning of the world to redeem and glorify people who would trust in God. God will not end this plan until it has been completed—by crowning with glory God's trusting children. And God's power is available every day to those who trust in Him.

Laying hold on these spiritual truths (wisdom) by faith leads to spiritual growth.

Questions for Thought and Discussion

(You may want to answer these questions personally in an essay, a meditation, or a praise song; or express through visual art what these truths mean to you. While you may prefer at first to answer the questions alone, you will find great value in sharing spiritual truths with others in the family of God. *Christian conversation* is a wonderful way to learn to talk aloud about these truths.)

1. Write out what the word *faith* has meant to you. Compare it with the definition in Hebrews. How does that definition help you to "mature" your own idea of faith?

2. When should we pray for spiritual wisdom? When we are in trials, or at other times? How does wisdom help us in everyday living?

3. Restudy the three phases of spiritual truth Ephesians 1 gives us. Express in your own way what these phases mean to you. How will they help you in your spiritual growth?

Personal Action Plans

Believing by faith that God is completely trustworthy and constant, I will

Exercising spiritual wisdom, "the mind of Christ" within me, I will

Affirming that God exists and answers my prayers, I pray that

Recognizing that God imparts wisdom as the never-failing source of power for living, I will

4

Growing in Power and Persistence

Power and persistence form the third couplet of elements of Christian growth. Compare these elements to some of the factors necessary in building construction. Whether the end result is a small cottage or a lofty skyscraper, some of the elements are the same.

A strong and secure foundation on which to build is the first necessity. Perhaps one of the reasons why Manhattan has some of the highest buildings in the world is that the island is on solid rock. Christians, too, have their "Solid Rock" foundation: Jesus Christ. Our relationship with Him as our Savior gives us a secure foundation for our lives in this world as well as in the next and provides the basis for our self-worth and integrity. A person who does not know basically who she is, or who God intends for her to become, can never fully develop her own personality in spiritual growth.

Next come the materials for the building: cement, wood, brick, metal, glass, plastic. You might compare these materials to faith and wisdom in the Christian life. These two elements provide, or make available, all the materials necessary for building a strong and beautiful life.

Take a closer look at the final couplet of elements of growth: power and persistence. You might compare power to all the sources of power used in building. You can compare persistence to the worker's contract to continue with construction until the job is complete.

Eventually we need to look again at the way all of these elements fit together. But first consider what the Bible says about power and persistence.

We Need Power for the Struggle

Ephesians 6:10–13

We do not often hear about the Christian's struggle against evil forces. Both the modern, secular rejection of belief in a personal devil and the present-day psychological understanding of life's problems have contributed to this neglect. Many people attribute their failures in life to parental/family influence, bad environment, and a corrupt society.

We have lost sight of the fact that all of these influences reflect the presence of evil in our world. Everything in life that is under the influence of God must contend with the forces of evil. The individual Christian's efforts to grow spiritually may and often do collide with the forces opposed to such growth. And that results in spiritual struggle.

Paul recognized this struggle and offered wise counsel about it (Eph. 3:10–18). He urged Christians not to attempt to fight in their own strength. Instead he advised believers to "be strong in the Lord and in the strength of his power."

How should we use this power? Every person in the Roman Empire was familiar with Paul's metaphor of the heavily armed soldier. Rome kept the peace by stationing soldiers in all parts of the empire. The foot soldier, with his armor, helmet, and sword, presented a formidable picture of the might of the empire. Christians have access to such might, Paul then said. A Christian soldier's job is more defensive than offensive. Christians need not hunt evil. They can be sure that evil will search them out. Christians, Paul said, need to be able to "withstand . . . and . . . to stand firm" (NRSV).

The armor Paul recommended for Christians is the armor of God. The emphasis in verse 11 is not on "whole," but on "of God." We do need the entire armor, but we need God's armor most of all. Isaiah 59:17 compares God to a soldier armed for battle. Paul may have had this verse in mind when he wrote Ephesians. At any rate, it is clear that Paul's emphasis was on the Christian's having the armor provided by and endorsed by God.

Notice how, over and over, Paul emphasized the word *stand* in these verses. The Christian's job is neither to run away nor to advance against the foe. The Christian's responsibility is to "stand firm." The devil's attacks will come thick and fast, and the devil has vast resources (v. 12). It is hard to know exactly what Paul meant by all these phrases. Perhaps he was not sure himself. But he did know that there is tremendous power in the attacks of evil. He wanted to warn his readers to be alert against attacks from any direction.

In verse 13 Paul encouraged the believers not only to "withstand" but also to "stand firm." A victory we win at the cost of disability or ultimate weakness to the victor is not total victory. What God promises to the Christian who struggles is this: If she takes the armor of God and is willing to be empowered with God's power, she will come through the struggle intact. Her victory, in God's strength, will be complete.

We Need Persistence to Finish Our Task

Hebrews 10:35–36

The previous passage raised the idea of persistence. This passage emphasizes it. The word *endurance* in Hebrews 10:36 carries the idea of a steadfast, unwavering persistence. This verse clearly states that endurance means continuing activity.

In verse 35 the writer to the Hebrews urged them not to "abandon" confidence in God. Perhaps they had gone through a period of trial and testing, and had come through victorious. This is the danger time—when the fighting is done and the struggler can relax. Then it is easy to wonder why the rewards of the struggle are not immediately forthcoming. We tend to teeter back and forth between strength and weakness, assurance and fear, highs and lows. The lows generally follow the highs. How often have you had a mountaintop experience quickly followed by a spiritual trough? The writer of Hebrews warned against this.

How did the writer say that we could conquer such a low? By endurance—by persistence. In verse 36 the writer reminded his readers that often a long gap of time exists between doing the will of God and receiving the promised reward. Chapter 11 remembers many of the heroes of God's faithful ones. In all these cases the reward did not come for many years, or did not come at all in the person's lifetime. Each "hero" is an example of persistence.

As Christians working at spiritual growth, we need the lesson of Hebrews 10:35–36. Growth is a long, slow process. Often we look for evidences of growth before they have had time to develop. Then it is easy to become discouraged. It is important to remember that God's time

40

is not ours. God works slowly but surely. In time, when we have done God's will, we will gain the reward. In this case the reward will be the beauty of Christlikeness, as Christ is being "formed in you."

We Need Assurance in Our Praying

Ephesians 3:14–16,20–21

As the climax to our focus on the three couplet elements of spiritual growth, look closely at a great prayer of Paul. The manner and assurance with which Paul prayed can be a means of deepening our own prayer.

Paul began by recognizing God as Father. The Creator of the universe is also Parent. God is the Father of our Lord Jesus Christ. Because Jesus trusted in God and was never disappointed in that trust, we can likewise depend on God.

God is also the Father Who gives name and sanction to "every family in heaven and on earth" (NRSV). The word *family* includes all social groups. God, the one true Parent, is the common head and original founder of every society. Because of this fact, we can look to our Father with increased assurance. God is concerned with us not only individually but also corporately. The greatest human society is the church. God, the Father of all societies, will not forsake that special group which is the body of Christ.

Verse 16 reminds us of the infinite resources of God. We have received some tokens of these resources, having learned something of the power of God in our lives. But these tokens are only a tiny portion of God's actual power. We see a pinpoint of light from a vast 100,000 light years away in space. This light can indicate, but never express, the total power of the gigantic star. So it is with our experience of the power of God.

Paul emphasized this point at the close of his prayer (v. 20). "Abundantly far more than all we can ask or imagine" (NRSV) is Paul's attempt to give some idea of God's ability to answer our prayers. All God's infinite resources are available to us, in accordance with God's will. And God's will (another term that is often found in the New Testament is "God's good pleasure") is that He shall be glorified, both in the church, the body of Christ, and in Christ, Who is the express image of the everlasting Father.

How does the church glorify God the Father? By becoming, corporately and individually, more like God's Son. As we grow spiritually into the likeness of Christ, we are bringing glory to God. Certainly, then, we can expect God to answer our prayers for power to grow spiritually.

Linking the Elements

Consider how the elements of spiritual growth are linked together. *Self-worth* helps us to know, appreciate, and accept who we are. We get from this a kind of blueprint of the way we can reflect Christ in our individual lives. Therefore we will ask for *wisdom* to work out that plan under God's guidance. *Integrity* causes us to stand in awe of God, lest we fall short of the divine will for us. Our integrity causes us to have *persistence* in carrying out God's will. *Faith* knows how to ask for *power* and *wisdom* and to believe that we will receive them. In this way, all of the elements of spiritual growth work together to build the Christian woman into the likeness of Jesus Christ, to the glory of God the Father.

Questions for Thought and Discussion

1. Where do you experience struggle in your spiritual life?

2. Paul described his spiritual armor in terms of the military of his day. How would you describe the elements of spiritual armor which you need?

3. What part of spiritual growth is hardest for you? What discipline do you need to grow in this area?

4. Look back on your life as a Christian. Where do you see evidence of growth? Where do you see need for more persistence?

Personal Action Plans

Accepting God's power in my life, I commit to stand firm in my struggle against

Believing in the faithfulness of God, I commit to persistence as I

Recognizing God's infinite resources, I pray for

5

Growing in Kindness and Friendship

This chapter and the following ones will focus on *areas* of spiritual growth. Kindness and friendship may seem elemental to you. They are. This is the reason we need to begin with them. In our eagerness to grow spiritually, we often begin with difficult areas, resulting in significant struggle. But progression in spiritual life, as in other areas, is from lower to higher, from the more simple to the more complex.

There is another reason why we should begin with kindness and friendship. It is usually easier for us to express affection to friends than to either family members or strangers. Within our families we are always busy with our roles: wife, mother, daughter, sister. We are not always able to be ourselves. But with our friends, especially our Christian friends, we can be more nearly who we are. Someone once said that a true friend loves—not in spite of the bad things, or because of the good things, in the other—but because she values the total person. Showing affection to friends is much easier than showing it to strangers. Loving with a minimum of risk comes before loving where there is a risk of hurt or rejection.

Jesus understood this principle thoroughly. He used it in giving His disciples His greatest commandment (John 13:34 NRSV): "'I give you a new commandment, that you love one another. Just as I have loved you, you also should love one another.'" Notice that Jesus did not say, "Love the world as I have loved you." He knew that they were not capable of laying down their lives for the world, as He was in the process of doing. He commanded total self-giving among the Christian fellowship. As we love each other with Christ's love and draw strength from giving and receiving that love, we can grow to love all people outside the Christian family.

The Tie That Binds

1 John 3:14–18

Did John have Jesus' commandment in mind when he wrote these words? John did not say so specifically. But it is hardly likely that he had forgotten it, even after so many years.

We can know what love really is, John said, because Jesus laid down His life for all people (v. 16). Wasn't this what Jesus had in mind when He commanded His disciples to "love . . . just as I have loved you"? Not every person will be required to lay down her or his life. But the ultimate test is our willingness to give up our lives for the sake of another whom we love.

Notice that here, even as in John 13, this test is not applied to love for everyone. John said that we ought to lay down our lives for those who are in the Christian family. It takes godlike love to lay down one's life for those who are enemies and sinners (Rom. 5:6–8). For human beings it is enough that we are willing to give up our lives for those who are our friends.

Loving others in the Christian family is the test of whether someone is alive spiritually, according to John (1 John 3:14). Why is this the test? Not because we are going to love our Christian friends perfectly. But the fact that we are able to love shows that the source of our life is in God, Who is love. Such love is energizing, life-giving.

John contrasted love with hate—that hate that issues in murder. Lack of love and concern for others lives next door to active hate. Such hate, the emotion that declares another person is not worthy of concern, opens the door to the destruction of that person. It is natural then to recognize the ultimate in love as the giving up of one's life. For the ultimate in hate is to take away another's life.

However, John did not demand that kind of self-giving as proof of love. Instead, he took the very practical step of caring for the immediate needs of another. It is often easier for us to declare our willingness to sacrifice our lives than it is to actually sacrifice some time, money, and effort to take care of the material needs of someone else. John knew that people would rather talk about great sacrifices than make small ones. So he warned his readers not to love in word alone. They should show their love "in truth and action." They were to perform deeds of kindness to their Christian friends. Such deeds must be "in truth," out of true caring.

The following Bible passages deal with the practical implications of this basic passage on love of others within the Christian family.

The Fellowship of Kindred Minds

Romans 12:10,15–16; 1 Peter 4:8–10
In these passages we find a number of practical suggestions for showing love toward one another. Notice that the basic statement in each passage relates to love: "Love one another with mutual affection; outdo one another in showing honor" (Rom. 12:10 NRSV). "Above all, maintain constant love for one another, for love covers a multitude of sins" (1 Peter 4:8 NRSV). This is reciprocal love, which receives while it gives. It is also the motivation for acts of kindness and friendship.

Romans 12 includes many such acts of reciprocal love. Look at a few mentioned in verses 10 and 15–16.

Those who love one another are eager to show one another honor or respect. Such honor is a balm to the spirit. Our culture generally discourages us from bragging on ourselves. Perhaps this is the reason that we have difficulty bragging on others. But friends know each other's good points and are eager to make them known. All of us can enjoy the honest praise of friends—and we should.

Mutual affection leads to mutual sharing of feelings (v. 15). This is easier than it sounds. We are often so locked up in our own emotions that we do not know how to enter into the feelings of others. But our love can lead us to feel the pains and sorrows of our friends.

A young woman had a dear friend whose father died suddenly of a heart attack. The young woman wished to sympathize with her friend but felt her lack of experience. So she cried out, "Oh, I wish I had lost someone, so that I could know how you feel!" This is true mutual affection. We do not always have the same experiences as our friends, but we can enter into their feelings as we forget our own.

Someone has said that it is easier to "weep with those who weep" than to "rejoice with those that rejoice." Envy, the desire to enjoy what the other has, cuts us off from rejoicing. But true love causes us to feel with the other person.

Such ability to enter into the other's feelings makes for harmony in the fellowship (v. 16). This includes living in harmony with those who are "lowly," or taking on humble duties. (The verse may have either meaning.)

Certainly it is important not to be conceited. The person who lives in love with her fellow Christians has less reason than others to be conceited. Conceit or egotism grows out of a lack of feeling one's self-worth. We have already discussed self-worth at length. Here it is enough to emphasize two reasons for the Christian's self-worth. First, she has her own unique nature, given to her by God and redeemed by Jesus as her Savior. Second, she has the warmth of being built up by fellow Christians.

People who receive honor, recognition, and unfailing sympathy from their friends have no need to puff themselves up. They can associate comfortably with other people regardless of social, economic, or other distinctions. In fact, they may find in these persons special qualities to admire which they never suspected. Also, they can take on whatever tasks need to be done without feeling a loss of worth.

The passage from 1 Peter contains more practical applications of brotherly love. Verse 8 says that "love covers a multitude of sins." We can understand this statement better if we look at Proverbs 10:12 (NRSV), from which it is apparently quoted: "Hatred stirs up strife, but love covers all offenses." Hate leads to strife and disagreements between people. Love leads to harmony by covering the sins of those involved. This does not mean ignoring the sins. But love's function includes caring about the total person, not just the part that is acceptable. So love, as it were, throws a blanket over the sins of the one who is loved. And isn't it true that such love brings the sinner to repentance far more truly than does condemnation? After all, Jesus did not come to the world to condemn the people in it, but to offer atonement toward repentance.

It is interesting that Peter made such a point of hospitality as an expression of love (v. 9). So did Paul, in Romans 12:13 as well as in other places. So did the writer to the Hebrews (Heb. 13:2) and John (3 John 5–8).

Hospitality was one of the most necessary services in the early church. There were no hotels. Inns were few,

48

scattered, and often not safe. Certainly they were of the most meager quality. People who had to travel usually arranged to stay with friends or relatives in distant cities.

There was much coming and going in the Christian community throughout the Mediterranean world. Travelers regularly needed lodging for a night or even longer. Since many of these people were cut off from relatives because of their new faith, they had to rely on their Christian family for hospitality. Such willingness to give room and board may have become a burden to some. Certainly Peter found it necessary to remind his readers to give their hospitality "without complaining."

The gift of the home was only part of what Christians could do for one another. They were also to use the "grace gifts" each had received from the Lord in the service of other Christians. And why not? God gives such gifts with the expectation that we shall use them. Where better to begin than within the Christian family?

Our Mutual Burdens Bear

Galatians 6:1–5

The first verse of Galatians 6 hooks into the last verse of chapter 5. There Paul warned against conceit, as he did in Romans 12. When we consider Roman culture, it is no surprise that the apostles continually had to warn against this problem. The Romans were proud people. They disdained any attitude that did not elevate the person in her own eyes and in the eyes of others. Urging Christians to shun conceit, pride, and self-glorification flew in the face of this cultural background.

In the light of this warning, Paul went on to give some principles for the treatment of Christians who had been "detected in a transgression" (NRSV) This word *transgression* means a falling by the way. It probably refers to a slipping out of close walk with the Spirit, leading to unforeseen sin. Such a person does not need condemnation but restoration.

Who can best do this ministry? Not the person who is conceited, but the one who has "received the Spirit." Such a person is a loving friend. She will not gloat over her erring friend. Instead, she will think of her own possible weaknesses. These will make her more sympathetic toward the other person.

Then Paul gave a great principle: "Bear one another's burdens, and in this way you will fulfill the law of Christ" (NRSV). A burden is a crushing load. It is not the weight of everyday stresses. It is the accumulation of extra problems that mount up until the person can hardly bear them. This is when she needs someone to come alongside her and help to carry the burden. One who does this fills out the law of Christ. This is a principle of living as Christ would have us live.

The one who bears another's burden when she or he has fallen by the wayside *restores* the other person. This word means to repair, prepare, make perfect. All of these ideas are involved in restoration.

Paul then directed a stern warning to those who were conceited, who would not consider their own temptations. Those who think they are *something* when they are *nothing* are the ones who are puffing themselves up. *Something* and *nothing* here refer to a person's attitude toward herself and toward her sinning sister or brother. Everyone is somebody. But no one is sufficient within herself so that she needs no one else. That is the meaning of this verse.

It is very human to judge ourselves by others. If someone is stronger than her sister, she may feel that this shows her superiority. But Paul declared that each person should judge herself by God's standard. Paul reminded his readers in Philippians 2:12–13 (NRSV), "Work out your own salvation with fear and trembling, for it is God who is at work in you, enabling you both to will and to work for his good pleasure." This verse should prompt each person to ask: Am I following God's plan in the work I am doing for God? If so, then she will have a legitimate "cause for pride." She does not have to put down someone else in order to feel good about herself.

Then Paul gave the second half of the principle he had started in verse 2. "All must carry their own loads" (v. 5). It is true that we can help to bear the burdens of others. But finally, each of us has her own load to bear. Here is a balance of privilege and responsibility. We receive help when we need it. But we have to carry our own load. The same is true of all Christians.

Questions for Thought and Discussion

1. How can you help to meet the needs of your friends, whether these needs are material, emotional, or spiritual?

2. Do you find it difficult to give honor to others? If you do, how do you need to change in order to be able to do so?

3. How well do you enter into the emotions of others or allow others to share your feelings? How can you become more open to others, in sharing feelings?

4. On a scale of 1 to 10, how would you rate how well you live in harmony with your friends? How can you change the number if it is too low?

5. How can you practice hospitality today, in spite of conditions much different from those in New Testament times? What other needs for warmth and acceptance can you meet?

Personal Action Plans

Recognizing that God, Who is love, enables me to show love to others, I will express love to _______________ this week by

Accepting my responsibility not only to "rejoice with those that rejoice" but also to "weep with those who weep," I will

Exercising my love for others, I will "bear the burdens" of _________ this week by

6

Growing in Mercy and Forgiveness

Perhaps one of the hardest actions of the Christian life is forgiving others—and ourselves—when we perceive that a wrong has been done. We are like the resentful people who say, "I'll forgive that person, but I'll never forget." We even find it hard to accept the total forgiveness of God. We may know intellectually that God forgives our sins, but we still beat ourselves over the head as we remember our shortcomings. How can we break the cycle of wrongdoing, resentment, attempts at forgiveness, and inability to put the past behind us?

An excellent insight comes from an English writer living in the fourteenth century. He is said to have described the mercy of God in this way: "He abideth patiently, he forgiveth easily, he understandeth mercifully, he forgeteth utterly."[1] Notice these wonderful attributes of God! Perhaps the most profound of these is that "he understandeth mercifully." God does not ignore our sins or cast them away without considering them. Rather, God plumbs the depths of human sins until God truly understands them. Then God applies to these sins the divine mercy: Seeing all the evil in the human heart and the repentance of the sinner, God is able to bestow mercy and to forgive and forget.

The passages for consideration in this chapter contrast human attitudes toward forgiveness with the "understanding mercy" of God. We may learn from these passages what keeps us from forgiving others and ourselves and the way we can move into the sunlight of God's forgiveness.

The Importance of Forgiveness

Matthew 18:21–35

Jesus used parables in His teachings as they fit the situation. Gospel narratives almost always give the settings for the parables. Often Jesus told a parable because someone presented a problem to Him. In Matthew 18 the setting of the story is clear. Jesus had been discussing the importance of forgiveness among believers (vv. 15–17). Peter had obviously been thinking of what Jesus had said. Impulsively he blurted out, "'If another member of the church sins against me, how often should I forgive? As many as seven times?'" (v. 21 NRSV). Peter seems to have thought that seven would be a generous number of times to forgive someone. So he must have been stunned to hear Jesus' reply: "'Not seven times, but, I tell you, seventy-seven times!" (v. 22 NRSV).

Then Jesus told the parable of the two debtors. He wanted to illustrate the truth that it is the quality, not the quantity, of forgiveness that is important. The attitude of mind that yields forgiveness does not count times!

The story grew out of a practice familiar to Jesus' listeners. The Roman Empire had many governors, petty kings, and small-time princes. Each held his position by permission of the emperor of Rome. They "governed" in only a limited way. Their main concern was the revenue they could get from the people under their reign. They parceled out their territory to lesser officials. Often these men were slaves, as in Jesus' parable. The responsibility of these persons was to collect the revenue due to the king and turn it over. Periodically the ruler would call his slaves in for an accounting. This is the way Jesus began His parable.

Evidently one of the king's slaves had been remiss in his stewardship. Either he had not collected all that was due to his master, or he had withheld the sums, thus becoming an embezzler.

It is pointless to inquire how he could have run up so vast a debt. Ten thousand talents was a great fortune, even in silver (money was calculated by weight, of either gold or silver). Jesus made the sum extravagantly large to show that it was impossible to repay. He also had the purpose of drawing a clear contrast between this debt and the one owed to the slave (v. 28).

When the king learned of the debt, he ordered that the man, his family, and all his property be sold. Certainly that would not have repaid the debt. But it was the best recompense the king could get.

Notice the slave's response. He did not ask the king to forgive him. Probably he felt that this was useless. The kings who lived by their countries' revenues could not afford to recklessly forgive others the debts they owed. The slave instead asked for time so that he could repay the debt. Of course, he could not have repaid it in his lifetime. But he was desperate; he would have offered anything.

Imagine his surprise, then, when the king acted utterly out of character. He was so moved by the slave's plea that he was overwhelmed with compassion. In the story it seems that the king acted spontaneously, on the basis of his merciful impulses rather than his hardheaded business sense. He forgave his slave the entire, vast amount that he owed!

Stop for a moment and imagine what thoughts and feelings the slave might have had. How would you have reacted to such a generous deliverance? The Bible does not tell us about his feelings, but his actions seem to speak clearly of his inner attitude. He went out and "came upon" a fellow slave. This man owed him a paltry sum, especially in comparison to the vast sum he had owed the king. A debt of $20 against $20 million might provide a modern-day comparison.

The slave who had had his debt forgiven immediately took drastic steps. He started choking his fellow slave, "seizing him by the throat." He was determined to get from the man what was owed him at once, no matter what means he had to use.

Notice the words of the fellow slave. They are word for word what the first man had said to the king (cf. vv. 29 and 26). Wouldn't you think the forgiven slave would have heard the echo of his own words so recently spoken? Apparently he did not. He showed no mercy at all. The tense of "pleaded" and "refused" in the Greek indicate repeated action. We can imagine that the fellow slave kept on pleading for time and the first slave kept refusing. At last the slave had his debtor cast into prison, with orders that he remain there until he or his family could raise the money.

The other slaves of the king were shocked by what they saw happening. In their distress they went to the king and told him fully of the incident. The king's anger was strong. He immediately had the forgiven slave brought before him.

One word in this speech (vv. 32–33) is noteworthy. It is the word translated "debt." The same word is used in verse 27. But this is not the same word in the Greek. The word in verse 27 means a loan. In verse 32 it means something owed, and may refer to a crime or offense. Obviously, in his first reading of the case, the king had decided to treat the official's debt as a loan to be written off the books. At the end he looked upon the debt as an offense, something to be paid for by pain and imprisonment.

Notice what the king condemned his slave for—it was for not adopting the same attitude the king had taken toward him (v. 33). Jesus summed up His teaching by a stern warning: "'So my heavenly Father will also do to every one of you, if you do not forgive your brother or sister from your hearts'" (v. 35 NRSV). Jesus' words emphasized the similarities of punishment as well as the similarities of attitude. He pointed out that anyone who had the attitude of the unforgiving slave would bring down on herself the punishment this man incurred.

Why did the slave not change his attitude? The Bible does not explain, but we can make some guesses. Getting an idea of the dynamics behind his actions may help us to avoid similar attitudes.

The slave seemed to be totally self-centered. He did not seem willing to put himself in his debtor's position. He heard his own words from the other man's mouth, but they did not register. Compassion calls for identification with the other, but he did not have it. Also, he did not seem to have learned from his own experience. He had not internalized what had happened to him. What may have been the reasons for his self-centeredness, his lack of profiting by his experience?

1. He may have discounted the king's merciful attitude toward him. He may have said, "He is so rich, he won't miss even that much money. But I'm a slave and poor. I've got to have what is owed to me."

2. He may have had a legalistic attitude. "If I let this guy get away with a small debt, what might he get into? I owe it to him not to make it easy on him."

3. He might have equated the other person's position with his own. He may have thought the other was being dishonest, as he himself had been. In that case, it would have again been the old proverb, "We condemn in others the sins we most despise in ourselves."

Whatever his reasons, it is clear that he did not understand or appreciate his master's attitude. Instead of becoming better because of his master's generosity, he became worse. The attitude of "give me what's coming to me" was hardening. If the king had not confronted him, we can imagine that in his later years this man would have become hard, uncompromising, and bitter.

This is the heart of Jesus' teaching about forgiveness: It is not what our unwillingness to forgive does to others so much as what this attitude does to us. Personal counselors recognize the importance of childhood attitudes and experiences. They have found that often a person's anger toward and unwillingness to forgive her or his parents carries over into adult life. Instead of continuing to be angry with the parent, the person displaces the anger onto others. He may be bitter toward his boss, who reminds him of his dominating mother. She may show anger toward her husband instead of her father. She may be envious of a co-worker who reminds her of her overachieving sister. In all these cases the root problem lies in unforgiving anger.

Parents often teach unforgiving attitudes to their children. They make the children work for forgiveness. They will not allow reconciliation without large doses of remorse. And the parents exhibit unforgiving attitudes toward others around them.

These attitudes keep people stuck in their relationships with others. They find it hard or even impossible to believe in the total forgiveness of God. They may spend their lives trying to earn the salvation God has already provided. Their growth as Christians is thus badly stunted.

The Process of Forgiveness

Psalm 103:8–14

How do we learn forgiveness, then? First, we need to recognize that for human beings forgiveness is more a process than an act. The act of forgiving becomes the final step in the process. The attitude of mercy toward others is the beginning. As we noted earlier, being able to "understand mercifully" leads at last to being able to "forget utterly."

Consider the perfect model of forgiveness: God. We are to forgive as God forgives us. How do we do that?

A favorite saying of a pastoral counselor friend, plus some new insights into Psalm 103:10–14 several years ago, helped bring me to a better understanding of God's forgiveness. My friend used to say, "To understand is to love, and to love is to forgive." This used to seem simplistic to me until one day I put it with Psalm 103:10–14. Then it made a heavenly lot of sense!

God's mercy and blessings are the theme of this psalm. Verse 8 states God's mercy and grace toward us. Verses 10–14 explain how these attributes work in relation to our sins. Verse 10 (NRSV) says that God "does not deal with us according to our sins." The verse reminds us of the merciful attitude of the king in Jesus' parable. The amount of the debt was of no concern to him in dealing with his slave. He would have been compassionate over a small amount or a large amount. This is how God acts, only in infinitely greater measure.

To see how the saying, "To understand is to love, and to love is to forgive," fits with God's model of forgiveness, look at the verses of this psalm in reverse order.

Verse 14 (NRSV): "For he knows how we were made; he remembers that we are dust"—understanding.

Verses 11,13 (NRSV): "For as the heavens are high above the earth, so great is his steadfast love toward those who fear him. . . . As a father has compassion for his children, so the Lord has compassion for those who fear him"—love.

Verse 12 (NRSV): "As far as the east is from the west, so far he removes our transgressions from us"—forgiveness.

God not only understands us thoroughly, He knows where we came from and what our limitations are. But God's understanding is also merciful. Knowing that we came from "dust," God does not expect perfection from us. God takes into account our frailties and has compassion on us. Likewise, we can understand one another enough to realize our mutual tendencies to failure. No one is so strong that she never needs compassion. No one is so perfect that she never needs forgiveness.

God loves us with the love of a parent—a father-mother. This is not the limited love of earthly parents. This is the total, giving, accepting love of a Parent Who understands totally and mercifully. We are in the process of learning more about that love. And how better to learn it than to practice it, so far as we are able!

Because God loves and understands, God forgives. That forgiveness comes from God's attitude of mercy toward us. This mercy, the psalmist said, is too great to be measured. It is high—as high as the heaven is above the earth.

The psalmist did not have the appreciation of space that we have. To him, the heaven above him was impenetrable. We know so much more today about our universe because of a space station from which we conduct observations and experiments. We can send probes to distant planets. But even as we reach out farther and farther beyond our own sphere, we find space stretching infinitely farther away from us. This is a picture of God's mercy: We cannot penetrate it or comprehend it. But we can follow it!

God's mercy leads to forgiveness of God's children. This is no light forgiveness. Notice how the psalmist described God's forgetfulness of our sins. God has put them as far away as the east is from the west (see v. 12). Think about directions on the earth. We can measure north and south quite accurately. There is a South Pole and a North Pole. We can get to absolute north at the North Pole. From there we start going south. But there is no way to measure absolute east and west. We arbitrarily speak of east and west. But if we go east far enough, we are in the west! In the same way God's mercy is infinite. We never get to the end of it.

We can follow this process of forgiveness in our relationships with our Christian brothers and sisters. When someone does us a wrong, we can begin by seeking to understand him or her "mercifully." We can ask: Why did my friend act this way? What old hurt, what twisted outlook, what past experiences have contributed to the hurt this person has done to me?

Once we begin to understand, even dimly, we can start to love. We will see this person, not as someone to be hated and to take revenge on, but as someone to be understood. She or he is like us, a being made of "dust." We will even see some of ourselves in this one's pains and problems. And who does not love herself? As we identify with the person who needs forgiveness, we learn more about loving our neighbor as ourselves.

In this attitude of mind we come to forgiveness. The mercy of God, which we have received, becomes active in our lives. We can forgive because we love.

The Practice of Forgiveness

Ephesians 4:31–32

As we look at the model of God's forgiveness, we can see why Jesus declared that our forgiveness of others is so important. Part of our spiritual growth is learning to forgive. The earliest knowledge we have of God is God's forgiveness and mercy. How will we ever learn much more about God if we neglect to learn God's forgiveness in practice?

Forgiveness and mercy make for healthy relationships. Instead of dumping on others the unforgiven hurts of our past, we can keep the channels between us clear. We will continually learn more of God as we practice God's kind of forgiveness.

How can we do this on a day-to-day basis? Look at Ephesians 4:31–32. There Paul set forth the negative and the positive sides of forgiveness. He urged his readers to get rid of their anger, bitterness, noisy strife, spite, harsh words. Of course, this too is a process. We don't overnight get rid of all our old patterns of behavior. But we can become aware of these patterns. Then we can consciously do away with them by recognizing their roots. Spite, bitterness, noisy arguments, harsh words, and anger are all patterns we have learned and practiced from childhood. If we learned these patterns, we can learn new ones.

We instill new patterns in our lives as we are kind, tenderhearted, and forgiving. Forgiveness, like friendship, begins with Christians. God for Christ's sake forgave the whole world. God asks us to begin by forgiving our Christian brothers and sisters as we have been forgiven by God. We take a step at a time in moving toward the ideal of God's forgiveness. And isn't it good that this is so?

---

[1]Thomas Merton, *Love and Living,* ed. Naomi Burton Stone and Brother Patrick Hart (San Diego: Harcourt Brace and Company, 1979), 205.

Questions for Thought and Discussion

(You can answer these questions more honestly with a sympathetic, understanding friend or in a small congenial group. If you plan to participate in a larger discussion group, you may find it better to make these hypothetical questions which can be considered impersonally.)

1. Put in your own words the phrase "understandeth mercifully." Would this be easy or hard for you? Which of your friends or relatives would you find it hard to "understand mercifully"?

2. Consider situations in which you might be like the unforgiving slave in Jesus' parable. What would it take for you to change your attitude in such situations?

3. Make a careful study of Psalm 103:10–14. Apply its truths to some relationship in your own life in which you find it difficult to forgive. How can you adopt God's attitude toward those who have wronged you?

Personal Action Plans

Recognizing that my unwillingness to forgive others stunts my Christian growth, I now resolve to forgive _______________ of

Acknowledging that forgiveness is more a process than an act, I will begin the process of forgiving _______________, showing mercy by

Affirming the fact that forgiveness and mercy make for healthy relationships, I will begin to replace negative patterns of behavior, such as anger, bitterness, strife, spite, and harsh words, with new patterns of behavior such as

7

Growing in Truth and Honesty

One of the most serious changes in public life today from earlier times is the tendency of trusted officials to lie or to tell only part of the truth. Everyone is very good at "shaving the truth" to make themselves look good. And it seems that no one ever admits to sin. "I made a mistake" seems to be the strongest statement of personal wrongdoing. Or else the person will try to mitigate individual failure by comparing it to other cases which are much more to be condemned. These evasions seem to pervade politics, business, education, and social institutions.

What has happened to the moral climate in our country? Is honesty no longer the best policy? And what about Christians? Do we live by the standards of the culture that surrounds us, or do we judge ourselves by the standards of the kingdom of God?

Early twentieth-century religious leaders used to say that the moral standards of society (at least, as they were proclaimed) were so much like those of Christianity that it was difficult to tell Christians from non-Christians. Now it seems that the standards of society affect Christians to a great degree. Sometimes it takes a lot of courage to fight against the lower standards of the persons among whom Christians live and work.

Truth and honesty are the measuring sticks by which much of our personal and social moral climate is judged. The Bible abounds with teachings regarding truth and honesty. Two of the Ten Commandments relate to these values. The prophets, from Elijah to Malachi, preached about honesty among people. Jesus had much to say about dealing honestly. Paul found problems in the early churches relating to these standards. It seems that for centuries, people have had problems with truth and honesty!

Out of this wealth of material, four Bible passages—Romans 13:3–8; Ephesians 4:15,25–29; Colossians 3:8–10; and Proverbs 30:8–9—form the basis for our thinking. All of them deal with truth in speech and honesty in actions. We will look especially closely at the verses pertaining to each subject. But we will need first to get a feel of each passage by putting it in the context in which it was written.

Paul wrote Romans as a letter to Christians in the church at Rome. He had never visited Rome, nor had he met many of these people. He was looking forward to knowing them personally. It was his ambition to "preach the gospel also . . . at Rome" (NRSV). His letter was a way of introducing himself to these Roman Christians, and he addressed concerns that he thought would apply to them.

Romans 13 is part of the "practical" section of Paul's letter. He seldom separated deep theology from everyday living. So, after he had finished the great chapters on faith and salvation (Rom. 1–11), he turned to the way Christians ought to live.

Paul made more reference to civic integrity in this letter than in most of his others. This may have been natural. The readers of his letter were mostly citizens of Rome, unless they were slaves or came from other parts of the empire. Paul may have been concerned that these

Christians might shirk their civic duties because they believed their loyalty belonged only to Christ. It is also important to realize that the Roman emperor at this time was Nero, certainly no model of a good ruler! And there was much corruption among public officials. Still Paul made his points about civic honesty.

Ephesians likewise combines deep theology with practical Christian living. The practical section begins with chapter 4. Paul evidently had two purposes in his remarks in that chapter: To promote the unity of the church (vv. 1–16) and to encourage his readers to break completely with pagan ways (vv. 17–32). The verses we will examine more closely deal with both of these purposes.

Colossians deals with the deep-seated heresy that was making inroads in the church at Colossae. In part, this heresy dealt with the worship of angels. It also called for keeping strictly to the Jewish laws. Paul wrote to the Colossians to condemn this heresy. Included in his instructions were the words we will examine more thoroughly. He was particularly concerned lest the Colossians fall back into their evil pagan ways.

Proverbs is usually called the proverbs of Solomon, although he likely did not write most of them. Agur wrote the proverbs that include the focal verses in this chapter. I, for one, am glad that Agur's proverbs are included, for his words contain some of my favorite Bible verses on the subject of money.

Having looked at the background of these passages, consider their teachings on truth and honesty.

Honesty in Citizenship

Romans 13:3–7

Paul's words to the Romans have a stern ring. He stressed respecting governmental authorities, keeping the law, and paying taxes! He declared that public officials had the power to enforce the law. Their purpose was to punish lawbreakers and thus to preserve peace and order. Paul called such an official "God's servant for your good" (NRSV). Not all government personnel claim to be religious, but they are God's servants just the same. Their offices exist to preserve order in society. And God is the King of kings, Whose rule preserves order in the universe. In that sense anyone who works for public order and tranquillity is God's servant.

Christians need to be subject to the law because of their Christian conscience, Paul said. "Because of wrath" (v. 5) refers to the wrath or punishment meted out by civil authorities for breaking the law. Christians should obey the law, not because they may get caught and have to suffer the consequences, but for conscience' sake. They obey because they know it is right. Paul went on to recommend other civic duties for Christians to do out of the same motive—"because of conscience" (NRSV). These included paying taxes and other public revenues, giving respect, and showing honor (vv. 6–7).

How do you pay your taxes? Gladly? (Not likely!) Grudgingly? Resentfully? Unhappily? Certainly we should pay our taxes honestly.

Paul's writings make it clear that Christians should have honest dealings with law and government. To reinforce this point, Paul laid down an important principle. Look at verse 8. This has been called the "unpayable debt." Paul's principle is that when one loves, she acts with consideration and concern for the other person's welfare and rights. Naturally, if everyone acted in this way, we would have no need for laws. But human society isn't organized around the principle of love.

For the Christian, however, living by the law of love can take much of the drudgery out of keeping the laws. If I am concerned about my neighbor's welfare in his car, I won't run a red light or crowd him on a freeway. If I take thought for my neighbor's rights, I won't infringe on them. Thus it is not necessary to worry all the time about keeping the laws. I can fulfill the law through living in love toward my neighbor.

Honesty with Possessions

Proverbs 30:8–9

Many people seem to have this attitude toward possessions: "What is mine is mine, and I won't share it. What is yours can be mine if I can lay my hands on it."

It seems that honesty and truthfulness, especially about money, have taken a nosedive in the past several years. Even charitable institutions are targets from which embezzlers take large sums. The stock market and bank dishonesties of the 1980s have seemed to spawn a disregard for the possessions and rights of others. As a result, the very rich have accumulated even more wealth, and the poor have seemed to grow poorer.

Proverbs 30:8–9 gives an excellent corrective to these attitudes. Agur's prayer was that he would have the possessions he needed to sustain life, but not too much. He prayed specifically to be delivered from both poverty and riches. We might paraphrase his words as "have a decent standard of living."

Poverty and riches represent two extremes that open the door to temptation to sin. Poverty, lack of elemental necessities of life, may cause a person to steal in order to live. Riches can become an open door to lack of dependence on God. "If I have all this, why do I need God?" may be the rich person's reasoning. In possessions and material considerations, a good balance is essential. And this balance is maintained by one's relationship to God. When we trust God to supply all our need, we can live with much or little. (Read Phil. 4:11–13.)

The "New Self" Calling for Truth

Colossians 3:8–10

The first part of Agur's prayer (Prov. 30:8*a*) was that God would remove falsehood and lying from him. Like most Hebrews, his concept of God was that God was in total charge of everything in life, both good and bad. So he felt it necessary to pray for God not to send temptation his way. But he also saw the importance of his embracing truth. The New Testament emphasizes positive, personal response to temptation. The call here is for Christians to turn actively away from falsehood and to practice truthfulness. Look at Colossians 3:8–10.

Paul called on Christians to get rid of old habits of mind and speech. The Greek for this verb in verse 8 implies that this was something they did when they confessed Christ. But they still needed to live out what they had done by daily deliberate decision. So "Do not lie to one another" employs a tense that means "continue to stop lying to one another." It is easier to decide to change habits than to actually make changes. But the decision is necessary before the habit will be changed.

Unity in the Church Built on Truth

Ephesians 4:15,25–29

In his letter to the Ephesians, Paul called for truthful dealings between Christians as the foundation for unity. Ephesians 4:15 (NRSV) recommends "speaking the truth in love" as part of the process of "growing up into Christ." The earlier verses of the chapter deal with the importance of unity in Christ's body, the church. It is interesting, therefore, that Paul singled out truthfulness as one of the essential elements for growing toward unity and maturity in Christ (vv. 13–16).

Verse 25 calls again for speaking the truth. Paul's reason for truthfulness between Christians was that "we are members of one another." Certainly all the parts of the body are open to one another. If the tooth hurts, it doesn't lie to the rest of the body, saying, "I'm all right." It clearly signals its condition through the pain it engenders. Paul declared that the unity of the members of Christ's body demands similar honesty.

Such candor includes even the negative emotion of anger (vv. 26–27). These verses seem to be a contradiction of Colossians 3:8. However, in that verse Paul was pointing to the ideal of cleansing one's inner being of habits of anger, malice, and slander. It is impossible to do away with anger completely. It is a basic emotion, just like fear, love, and sadness. There are times when we feel anger.

When such times come, Paul seems to say that the appropriate response is to admit the anger and deal with it. In the context of truthfulness, the healthy way of dealing with anger is to express it, not to bottle it up and deny it. People do much more harm by hiding anger than by expressing it appropriately when it comes. Such expression should not be in the form of physical violence or hurtful words. It is appropriate to say simply, "I am angry with you because . . ."

The next step is to finish the anger—to get rid of it—as soon as possible (before the sun sets). We can finish anger through reconciliation with the other person or persons involved. If that is not possible, then we can resolve to let it go. Or we can let it out with friends who understand the situation and then let it go. But it is most important not to harbor anger. That leads only to hidden resentment and a breakdown of unity.

In verse 29 Paul made a recommendation for promoting unity through speech. He urged the kind of talk that is "useful for building up." What kind of speech builds up? Certainly it must be truthful. But it should also be kind and loving ("speaking the truth in love").

Most people, including Christians, spend a lot of time in trivial talk. While this may not be harmful, it is not positively helpful. We have neglected the art of "Christian conversation." In Christian conversation members of Christ's body share their joys and sorrows, talk about what Christ has done for them, and exchange new insights into spiritual truths. Such conversation need not always be serious. As Paul said, it should "fit the occasion." So humor, fun, and light talk have their place. What Paul insisted on was a balance suitable to building up the members of the body.

Questions for Thought and Discussion

1. Do you believe that it is possible for committed Christians to have an effect on the trend toward dishonesty in our society? How can such a small group change a large mass of people?

2. What did Jesus mean in Matthew 5:13–16 when He compared His followers to salt and light in the world (see also Mark 9:50 and Luke 14:34–35)? How can we be salt and light in the matter of truthfulness and honesty?

3. Review the principles of truth and honesty these Bible passages present. How can you put them into practice in your own life? What are you willing to do about it?

Personal Action Plans

Recognizing my responsibility to be an honest citizen in my community, nation, and world, I will

Acknowledging the need for balance in my life in terms of money and material possessions, I will

Affirming God's desire that I get rid of old habits of mind and speech in my life, I will

Affirming God's desire that I admit anger and deal with it honestly and appropriately, the next time I am angry with someone I will

8

Growing in Gratitude and Generosity

A dear friend of mine, a young pastor's wife, was discussing with me the many acts of kindness the church had extended to her and her family since they moved to their new church. "The problem is," she said, "that everyone keeps doing things for us. I thought they'd slack off after the first few weeks. But we've been here a year, and they're still bringing pies and cakes and inviting us out to dinner."

"What's the problem in that?" I asked, amused.

"It's just that I can't find any way to pay back all those people. I can't invite them all over to dinner or do special things for them. But I feel uncomfortable unless I can give them something back."

"Why can't you simply tell them thank you sincerely and let it go at that?"

She looked steadily at me, her brown eyes troubled. "Well, you see, that's what is hard for me. I was always taught, 'It is more blessed to give than to receive.' So, unless I'm giving, I don't feel as if I'm doing right."

I said to her gently, "You've learned the grace of giving, but not the grace of receiving. Why can't you let those kind people have the joy of giving to you without your having to 'pay it back'?"

Her look was startled now. "I have never thought of that! I didn't realize I was taking away their satisfaction in giving. Of course, I know that I don't want things in return when I give. But I never thought of other people feeling that way."

Sometime later, when I saw her again, she said to me, "I've really started saying just thank you and meaning it. It's still hard to do, but I have noticed how pleased people are when I respond with simple gratitude."

Most people who grow up in Christian homes and churches learn the grace of giving far more than the grace of receiving. "God loves a cheerful giver" (2 Cor. 9:7 NIV). "'It is more blessed to give than to receive'" (Acts 20:35 NIV). We learn these Bible verses early in life. Offertory responses, hymns, and admonitions to give generously resound in our ears. Who teaches us the grace of simple gratitude? Yet the clear message of the Bible is that generous giving is the natural outgrowth of gratitude to God for the bountiful gifts from God's own hand.

Sometimes we get the idea that we give to God first and then receive from God. This emphasis may surface during a stewardship campaign. But it is not that way. God gives to us before, during, and after we give. God gives to us whether we give or not. The more we learn to appreciate our heavenly Father's gifts, giving God true gratitude, the easier it will be to give to all people in God's name.

Lives Steeped in Gratitude

Colossians 3:14–17

Three times in these brief verses some form of the word *thanks* appears. Were the Colossians naturally grateful, so that Paul was affirming a general practice? Or were they ungrateful and he found it necessary to call them to thanksgiving? Neither extreme seems to be true. Rather, special circumstances in the Colossian church may have called out Paul's emphasis on gratitude.

Heretical teachers, who seemed to promote a combination of mystery religions and Jewish ceremonial practices, had influenced members of this church. As a result, these Christians were in danger of falling back into paganism. They were disturbed over the most elemental activities, such as tasting and touching certain things. They were losing the joy of their relationship with Christ (see Col. 1–2).

Epaphras, one of their ministers, had brought news of the church's situation to Paul. This letter was Paul's call to the Colossians to reaffirm their original relationship with Christ.

After discussing the doctrine of the supremacy of Christ, Paul turned to the quality of life this doctrine calls for. Chapter 7, "Growing in Truth and Honesty," focuses on some of these admonitions. Paul's major emphasis in those verses was on a changed life growing out of a changed nature. Paul completed this teaching in Colossians 3:14. He called for the Colossians to "clothe" themselves with love as one would bind a sash or girdle around one's waist to hold loose-fitting garments close to the body. Then he turned to the way the community needed to build itself up, as individuals lived out their inner change of nature.

Verse 15, then, is a transition. Paul spoke of the way the peace of Christ should rule in individual hearts, while calling attention to the fact that these Christians were all one body. Then he said, "Be thankful" (NIV). Thankful for what? Actually, Paul's words were, "Become thankful." It is not clear just what Paul meant by these words. But we can think of some possible meanings.

This section of Colossians sums up Paul's exposition on the changes Christ brings in individual lives through the new relationship with Him (see Col. 3:1–4). Perhaps Paul felt that the Colossians had been deeply troubled by what seemed to them like weighty responsibilities. This may have caused them to lose sight of their privileges as Christians. "Become thankful" may have reminded them of that glorious state of reconciliation with God through Jesus Christ.

Or Paul may have meant: You don't have to spend all your time going through rituals in order to satisfy God. God has already changed you inwardly through the Holy Spirit. Be thankful that this is so. Get your heads out of the sand of your worry. Exchange your fears of not doing everything right for the joys of a secure relationship with Christ. Become thankful rather than anxious.

Verse 16 deals with the relationship of Christians in their community of worship, study, and praise to God. Here, too, Paul called for thankfulness. What is the basis for this gratitude?

Paul believed that right kinds of study and praise would be a corrective for the false teaching that the Colossians had received. He urged them to steep themselves so thoroughly in the Word of Christ that they could teach one another "in all wisdom." They would not need the so-called wisdom of the mystery religions. They would have all the wisdom they needed from the teachings of their Lord. "Teach" here refers to doctrine. "Admonish" refers to instruction in the way to live. The Word of Christ provides the basis for both.

The Word of Christ is also the basis for praise to God through the singing of spiritual hymns. Song has been a vital part of Christian worship since its beginning. The joy of a right relationship to God wells up in the Christian's heart in thankfulness. It overflows in music, whether the person can sing well or not. Music is the joy of the heart made vocal. So Paul reminded his readers that they could sing with thankfulness.

Paul then summed up everything he had been saying in this chapter with a general recommendation to express thankfulness in every aspect of life (v. 17). Notice how comprehensive this verse is: "In word or deed . . . do everything in the name of the Lord Jesus, giving thanks to God" (NRSV).

How can we carry out such a suggestion? Wouldn't it be impossible, before every word or act, to weigh consciously whether we were doing it in the name of Jesus? And how can we constantly stop in our lives to give thanks to God?

Such questions—and probably most of us have raised them—show that we do not understand Paul's intent. His whole approach to the Christian life was that it should be the outgrowth of inner change. He had called his readers to give preference to the new life within them, thus stifling old impulses. Then he had called them to the mutual encouragement of worship and study together.

Out of these springs of action, corporate and individual, would come a new way of living. This way would make it possible to do all things in the name of the Lord Jesus. The more we know about Jesus, the more we love Him and seek to live as He did. The more we live in His name, the more truly we live as He revealed Himself to be.

Such a life is creative, joyful, growing, loving, courageous, energizing, winsome, integrated, and wise. We see these qualities in Jesus, and He inspires them in us. Who would not be grateful for such a life? It is an overflowing life that stands in glorious contrast to an existence without Christ.

Some Christians may say, "That's all very well for former pagans, like the Colossian Christians. But I have never been like them. I grew up in a Christian home. I don't know how to live any other way." It is true that people tend to live out in maturity the habits they formed in a Christian home. But even the best kind of moral life is purposeless unless it is linked to the vast purposes of the kingdom of God. Our relationship to God through the Savior Jesus is what counts. Those who try to substitute a moral life for a daily relationship with God do not really have much for which to be thankful.

The Boundless Circle of Giving and Receiving

2 Corinthians 9:6–12

Paul saw giving and receiving as two parts of a great wheel. Always revolving, it moves outward to give and inward to receive. Such actions are all part of the great interaction of the universe. God gives bountifully to His children, asking no return. God's children give bountifully to others, asking no return. And all—those who receive from God and those who receive from God's children—overflow with gratitude to God, the ultimate Giver.

These verses are full of superlatives. Paul seemed determined to give his Corinthian readers as exalted a picture of giving as he could. So he piled up descriptive words: *bountifully, every, in abundance, multiply, increase, in every way.* We get an overpowering impression of superabundance when we look at the words Paul used, especially in the Greek.

Paul's immediate concern was for the Corinthians to follow through on their pledges to help the impoverished Judean Christians. Perhaps some of the Corinthians had become reluctant to pay their pledges. Their income might have been less than they expected. They may have thought they had been rash in pledging a large amount. Whatever the cause, Paul was aware of it. Instead of scolding them for their change of heart, he sought to inspire them. He urged them toward great generosity growing out of great gratitude for the abundance that had been—and was being—showered on them by God.

To get the full impact of Paul's statements, we need to look at some of the words very carefully.

In verse 6 Paul began to develop his thesis. He compared giving and receiving to sowing and reaping. One ancient commentary puts it this way: "To give is not to lose but to sow seed." This was obviously the way Paul viewed the matter. He said that sowing (giving) sparingly leads to a sparse harvest (return). The word translated "bountifully" is derived from a Greek word meaning praise or benediction.

In verse 7 Paul reminded his readers that they had already made a commitment to give. Now they should carry through on that commitment. Their attitude should not be grudging or resentful. After all, they had not been forced to give.

Then Paul made the statement that is so familiar to us: "God loves a cheerful giver." Why does God love a cheerful giver? Because God is more concerned with our lives than with our gifts. God has untold riches upon which to call in order to help those in need. But God wants the people of God to know the joy of giving. Without joy a gift is bare.

Verse 8 goes on with the argument Paul began in verse 6. Notice the way verse 8 piles up the "every's." In how many ways is the richness of God's giving stated!

Paul quotes from the Old Testament in verse 9—Psalm 112:9. Verse 10 partly quotes from Isaiah 55:10. Paul was making the point that generous giving was no new idea with God and for God's people. In fact, it went back to God's law (Deut. 15:7–11). The prophetic writings, the psalms, and the proverbs repeated this idea many times. Of course, Jesus emphasized giving (see Matt. 6:1–4; 10:8, for example).

But Paul reminded his readers that even the means for giving the gift come from God (v. 10). Again we see how the wheel of giving turns. The seed, the means of giving, comes from God. When the seed produces a rich harvest, there is much bounty out of which to give—which leads to another sowing of seed.

Verses 11–12 pile up the superlatives just as verse 8 does. Notice how generosity and gratitude are intermingled in these verses. The greater the gift, the greater the thanksgiving to God. The greater the gratitude, the greater the generosity.

How Small a World!

Consider the difference between Paul's world and ours. Paul's was a small world, bounded on all sides by the Mediterranean Sea. But communication was quick, for that day. Travel by land and water was frequent and often fairly rapid. So it was easy for Paul to get news of the famine in Judea and the consequent suffering of Judean Christians. His response was equally speedy. He decided to take up an offering among the Christians in other parts of the Roman world to help supply food for their brothers and sisters in Judea.

Think about our world. It is not bounded by anything. We know about what goes on in the whole world in the twinkling of an eye. We can see famine in Africa, civil war in Europe and India, natural disasters from China to Central America.

What will be our response? Do we have the same concern for hungry persons in other parts of our world that Paul did? How can we most usefully help these people?

Questions for Thought and Discussion

1. Think of what God has done for you in extending salvation to you. How different is your life because you gave your life to Christ? What do you owe Jesus Christ in gratitude for this new life He has given you?

2. Think of Paul's words in 2 Corinthians 9. Can we take them seriously? Can we rely on God to provide the seed for our own welfare if we scatter our means lavishly to those in need?

3. How can we best show our gratitude to God for our safe and secure life? What obligation do we have to persons in need whom we will never meet?

Personal Action Plans

Acknowledging my gratitude to God, I will express thankfulness to God and to others this week by

Recognizing the world's great need, God's endless supply, and my eternal gratitude to God, I will give ______________ this week to help ______________

9

Growing in Concern for Those Without Christ

One of the greatest concerns of the Christian should be for persons whose lives are not related to God. We speak of such persons as "the unsaved," "the lost." But what do these terms mean? Do they convey real meaning to the persons with whom we may be concerned?

Look at these words as persons outside the church might look at them. They might ask: "What am I supposed to be saved from? How am I lost?" In the days of revivals in all the churches, preachers and evangelists gave definitions for the words *saved* and *lost*. Too often they meant being saved from hell, or lost to eternal death. People don't often think in those terms anymore. So it may help us to redefine them, for our own sake as well as for the sake of those to whom we seek to witness.

Being lost, in biblical terms, means to be out of relationship with God. In the parables of Luke 15, that is what lost means. The lost sheep had lost contact with the shepherd. The lost coin was not in the possession of its owner. The lost son had estranged himself from his father. So lack of meaningful relationship with God may be the essence of being lost.

What has caused this lack of meaningful contact? Doesn't God want to relate to us? The whole Bible shouts the answer, "Yes!" The Bible itself is the record of God's actions toward human beings. God has always been breaking through to human beings and establishing relationships with them. But why, then, doesn't God see to it that everyone comes to know Him in a meaningful way?

The answer lies in two places: in our free will and in God's consistent nature. People, through their own free will, choose to look elsewhere than to God for meaning and relationship. God will not drag people into relationship, nor will He overlook their rebellion. To do either would not be in God's nature. What God has done is far better. God determined to show what He is like by sending the Son, one just like God, to live among us and die for us. The depth of God's love and care for human beings was shown clearly in Jesus' love and care—even to the point of dying for us.

Still, the decision is up to each person. She may look in the wrong place for meaning and purpose. Deciding that west is east, she will continue to march in that direction, no matter what evidence may come to tell her that she is wrong. God works patiently, in many ways, to convince such a person that true life rests in God alone. How God has done this is called the message of reconciliation.

The Basis of Concern

2 Corinthians 5:17–20

God broke into history in the coming of Jesus Christ. Those who accept Christ as Savior and Lord of their lives have an experience so transforming that it is truly becoming a "new creation" (v. 17). The old existence has "passed away." And with excitement Paul said, "See, everything has become new!" (v. 17 NRSV).

How does this happen? It is "from God." In Jesus Christ, God perfected a plan whereby all human beings of all the centuries can be reconciled to God. This is on

God's terms, not ours. The result is that we will have the relationship and the purpose for which we have been searching.

Notice that this reconciliation is "through Christ." But even more, "in Christ God was reconciling the world to himself" (v. 19 NRSV). In Christ we see what it truly means to be in relationship with God, as a child is with her loving parent. And in Christ, God allowed the wrong human ways of living to come to culmination in the Cross. All the warped decisions of people combined to nail Jesus to the Cross. Then God validated what Jesus had done by raising Him from the dead. In so doing God made it clear that Christ's way is the way of ultimate purpose—to have eternal life, a "new creation" for those who give their lives to Jesus Christ.

Surely this is a message to give to all people! It counters all the willfulness and rebellion in us. It shows us that we can relate to God. It shows us how to relate by giving our lives over to God's Son. It tells us that we can turn around, find the true "east" of life, and walk in relationship with God through Jesus Christ.

One of the best things about this message is that in reconciliation God is willing to wipe the slate clean of a person's rebellion against God. No wonder this relationship can be called a new creation! It is like being born as a baby is born, with a completely new start.

The basis of concern is our knowledge, through experience, of what God has done for us. This knowledge cries out to be shared. Paul called those who witness to the new life in Christ "ambassadors for Christ." An ambassador carries messages from her government to foreign governments. She must be sure that she delivers these messages accurately and persuasively. She must have tact and diplomacy to deal with people of a different nationality and culture. She must believe in her government and in what she is doing.

So Paul spoke like an ambassador when he said, "We entreat you on behalf of Christ, be reconciled to God" (v. 20 NRSV). In this one sentence are all the qualities of the true ambassador for Christ. We see the concern of that ambassador that others may respond to the message. The free will of human beings is not overpowered. God will only beseech through the ambassadors. But God has done everything necessary to make reconciliation possible. The rest is left up to the ambassadors and to the power of the Holy Spirit working in the hearts of both the witnesses and those who need the witness.

The Debt of Concern

Romans 1:14–16

Suppose your child has a rare disease. You search in vain for years for a cure. Finally you hear of a treatment. You take your child to the clinic, and after a period of treatment she is cured. How would you feel about spreading the word of this great treatment? Wouldn't you want others to know about it? Wouldn't you feel an obligation to pass on the word to others who were suffering as your family had?

This illustrates what Paul was saying in this passage. He was so overwhelmed with the power of the gospel that he felt impelled to share the news about it to everyone. His urgency about sharing the gospel is an example to us.

The Attitude of Concern

1 Corinthians 9:19–22

Having concern that all people hear the gospel is not enough. We as Christians must be concerned for individuals. It is not enough to hand out leaflets about salvation. Witnessing can never be a mass endeavor. When we witness, we tell someone else what Christ means to us and how our relationship with Him has changed our lives.

Paul always remembered the individual in his witnessing. He explained his attitude in this Scripture passage. When he was with Jews, he followed their customs. When he was with Gentiles, he abandoned Jewish ways and accommodated himself to the Gentile lifestyle. But he was always true to himself. He said that he was always under the law of Christ. By that he meant that he did not do anything that would violate his own standards of conduct. But where there were customs that did not make any real difference, he fitted in with the people. He did not give them the impression that he was condemning their customs.

This was the same principle that Jesus followed. He ate meals with tax collectors and prostitutes. He visited them in their homes. But He did not follow their moral standards. By accepting them as individuals, He was able to communicate God's love to them.

This is the principle we must follow, if we are to lead others to trust their lives to Jesus Christ. It is often easy for us to look at the way people live and condemn them. Or we may not recognize their desire for God because we are so busy looking at their lifestyles. Both Jesus and Paul looked at the positive in people and related to it. Then they were able to move on to point these people to the truth of God's love.

The Far Reach of Concern

1 Timothy 2:1–6
We have been thinking mainly of expressing concern in personal contacts. But what about people we may never see? This is the realm of prayer. Paul had much to say about praying for others. In this passage he gave some

excellent directives for praying for those beyond our personal reach.

Paul gave a direct order to Timothy to be sure that his church people prayed for everyone. Three times in these verses Paul makes reference to all people. Christians are to pray for all persons (v. 1). It is God's desire for all human beings to be saved (v. 4). Christ gave His life as a ransom for all people (v. 6). We should pray for all persons because God desires for them to be saved, and Christ gave His life for all people. There is no suggestion here that any one group is more deserving of prayer than another. There is no separation of human beings into racial, ethnic, or social groups. There is no recognition of friendly or unfriendly groups. All people deserve our prayers.

Then Paul said something even more startling. He commanded that "kings and all who are in high position" (v. 2 NRSV) should have special prayers. It is important to recognize that this letter to Timothy was probably written during the reign of the infamous emperor Nero. Dark clouds were gathering on the horizon for Christians. Paul did not say that these rulers should be those whose ways Christians would approve. Certainly, neither Paul nor any of the first-century Christians would have found anything to admire in Nero! Yet Paul commanded prayers for him and for all government officials. Paul had a specific reason for this command. It was "that we may lead a quiet and peaceable life" (NRSV).

How does this reason fit in with his next statement, that God approves such praying? There are many reasons, but the one that leaps to mind as we consider the spread of the gospel is this: It is in tranquil times that missions work goes ahead with more power. Whenever there is civil war, wars between nations, national unrest, or disaster, the work of missions and missionaries is hindered.

There is much work to be done during such times, but the immediate needs of the people are so great that the work of witnessing and church starting must wait.

So God approves of our praying for stable government and for times of peace and tranquillity. In these contexts we will not only live with more assurance of mind but we will also be in a position to spread the word of God's reconciliation to all people. As we recognize that there is one God and one mediator, we know the importance of praying for all. Through our prayers we may reach into the farthest areas of the world. God created us. We all need God. God made provision for the salvation of all. It is our task to spread the gospel to all.

Questions for Thought and Discussion

1. What is your level of concern for persons who have not been reconciled to God? On a scale of 1 to 5, with 5 representing the highest level, rate your concern for these persons:

    Family member or close friend
    Co-worker
    Neighbor
    Street person
    Casual acquaintance

2. How can you raise your level of concern, if it's below 3?

3. What is your attitude toward persons who are different from you because you are a Christian and they are not?

4. How real to you are the people in "faraway places" whom you will never see? How can you make your prayers for them more personal?

5. How do you think you should pray for persons in government work? What kind of prayers will help them most?

Personal Action Plans

Acting out of the knowledge of what Christ has done for me, and on the basis of my concern that others share this gift, I will serve as Christ's ambassador by

Accepting my responsibility to spread the gospel to all people, I commit to pray regularly for the salvation of

10

Growing in Love

Love belongs at the beginning of the Christian pilgrimage. It is through God's love that we become Christians. We might think of love as the center of spiritual growth. Paul put it this way: "Love does no wrong to a neighbor; therefore, love is the fulfilling of the law" (Rom. 13:10 NRSV). So why has it taken us ten chapters to get to love as one of the elements of spiritual growth?

Love is the climax. In the list of "add to's" in 2 Peter 1:5–7, love is the last element in the list. Paul listed love as the foremost of the fruits of the Spirit (Gal. 5:22). It is in this sense that we now consider love.

Paul gave a beautiful word picture of the function of love in Colossians 3. In *The Complete Bible: An American Translation,* Edgar Goodspeed's translation shows this word picture very clearly: "You must clothe yourselves with tenderness of heart, kindness, humility, gentleness, forbearance. . . . And over all these put on love, which completes them and fastens them all together" (Col. 3:12,14).

In this chapter we will explore three aspects of love: its source, in God the heavenly Parent; our experience of it, through Jesus the Son; and its power in our lives, through the Holy Spirit.

The Source of Love: God the Heavenly Parent

1 John 4:9–10,16,19

The first Bible verse many children learn in Sunday School is "God is love." The source of all love in the universe is God—the heavenly Parent, the Giver of Life, the Infinite, the All-Powerful Nurturer, Encourager. Our ability to love comes from God, both directly and indirectly. God loves us directly and makes it possible for all human beings to love. It is interesting that love is not an inborn instinct; yet we all need love to survive.

In a study of infants who had to be in a hospital over an extended period, especially those who were born prematurely, it was found that those who had little human contact, such as patting and holding, tended to be weaker and to get sick more easily than those who were held and caressed. It was concluded that emotional deprivation—the withholding of love—had a bad effect on the very young child.

Every child needs love in order to develop emotionally and physically. We cannot give love unless we have received it. In 1 John 4:19 (NRSV) we read, "We love because he first loved us." Our very ability to love comes from the fact that God loves us. And God loved us before we could do anything to merit that love. A human example is the way parents love their children long before they can do anything to deserve such love. A child exists; therefore, she is loved. In this same way God loves every human being God creates.

What is the quality of God's love? Verses 9–10 answer this question. God's most powerful expression of love came when Jesus Christ was sent into the world "so that we might live through him." God's gift of love was not just in sending the Son of God to live among us. God "did not withhold his own Son, but gave him up for all of us" (Rom. 8:32 NRSV). God did not turn away from Jesus when He was nailed to the Cross. No! God participated in the agony of the Son. God's love goes the distance. It leaves nothing undone that could bring human beings to God.

As we respond to God's love with our love, our whole lives change. We live in God, and God lives in us. It is like having an electric current continually flowing between God and us. There is a constant exchange of love and communion between God and us (see v. 16).

The Experience of Love: God the Son

Ephesians 3:17–19
We considered most of this magnificent prayer in chapter 4 when we focused on power and persistence. But these three verses contain the heart of the prayer. Its theme is the experience of the love of Christ.

"Dwell" is an interesting word here. Its meaning is "to take up permanent residence." Christ's presence in the lives of His people is not a temporary, on-again, off-again matter. When Jesus Christ moves in, He does so permanently.

Paul then went on to speak of being "rooted and grounded" in love. Actually "grounded" is "founded" in the Greek. It refers to the foundation of a building. So the meaning here is "being securely rooted like a plant and being solidly based like a building" on divine love.

What do we see when we see "the breadth and length and height and depth" of God's love? W. O. Carver put it this way: The breadth is "extending to all peoples." The length is "all time." The height is "to the very presence of the Supreme God." And the depth is "to the lowest condition of human need."[1]

When I was a young woman I heard my pastor link this verse to John 3:16 as a way of explaining it. He did it this way: "For God so loved the world [the breadth of God's love], that he gave his only begotten Son [the length to which his love would go], that whosoever believeth in him should not perish [depth], but have everlasting life [height]."

There are many other ways of looking at all the dimensions of God's love through Christ. Perhaps you have your own way. None of us can truly comprehend that love. But as we consciously place ourselves in the center of God's love, we will progressively come to know more and more of it.

This, too, was what Paul prayed for—that his readers might "know the love of Christ that surpasses knowledge" (NRSV). How can this be? How can we ever know what is beyond our knowledge? The knowledge of which Paul was speaking comes by experience. It is similar to the way one friend knows another. The more understanding that comes, the more there is to learn. This is infinitely true with Christ.

Paul was always praying for seemingly impossible things! His reason was that he knew enough about God to be sure that God's resources would always be far beyond anyone's ability to exhaust (see v. 20). So Paul's final prayer was set in the realm of the impossible also: "that you may be filled with all the fullness of God" (NRSV). Paul's prayer was that Christians should be filled up to the measure of the infinite God.

Paul was not speaking here of individual Christians. He was speaking in the plural, of the church as Christ's body. Only as the whole body of Christ can we come to experience the love of Christ in its fullness. Even that is partial and progressive in this life. Paul's prayer will only be answered in its fullness when all God's people experience God fully in eternity.

The Power of Love: God the Holy Spirit

1 Corinthians 13:4–7

The Holy Spirit is not mentioned in this great "love chapter," but the Spirit's presence there is unmistakable. As was mentioned earlier, the foremost fruit of the Spirit is love. Without the indwelling power of the Holy Spirit, the characteristics of love spelled out in these verses would be impossible to attain.

The perfect example of the characteristics of love is Jesus Himself. We could read 1 Corinthians 13:4–7, substituting the name of Jesus for the word *love*. Each reference would be fitting. We would have a perfect picture of love seen in a human being.

These qualities of love are so comprehensive that they are hard to grasp. I always used to think that 1 Corinthians was a magnificent poem to the beauties of love. Then for the first time I read the chapter in a modern-day translation. "Vaunteth not itself, is not puffed up" and all the rest, as rendered in the antique language of the King James Version, were just pretty words. But when I read, "Love is not jealous or boastful; it is not arrogant or rude" (v. 4 RSV), I had a feeling of intense discomfort. Those words were pointing straight at me. Instead of a poem, 1 Corinthians 13 became a measuring stick, and a very hard one.

It is a good idea, I think, to read this chapter in as many translations as possible. The word pictures are vivid. Different translations give particular emphasis to different qualities. To get something of the flavor of this passage, take a look at each quality of love separately.

Patient. This is not the patience of persistence but the patience of relationship. It means long-suffering. In the Greek the word translated "patience" is made up of two elements, one meaning "long" and one meaning "wrath."

The combination would be the opposite of our expression *short-tempered*. The patient person doesn't "fly off the handle." It takes a long time for her to get mad.

Kind. This involves doing friendly and useful acts for another. The kind person avoids an attitude of criticism or self-righteous judgment. Rather, she constantly seeks the good of the other.

Not envious. This means not begrudging the success or the good fortune of others. Such a person is happy to rejoice in what another owns or has accomplished, even though she may not share in the good fortune.

Not boastful. This is the parallel to not being envious. The one who has things of which to be proud does not brag about them. She is careful not to rouse the possible envy of others.

Not arrogant. This involves not being inflated with a sense of one's own importance. Such persons are often insecure in themselves. They "puff themselves up" because they fear no one will notice them otherwise. But love knows no such insecurity.

Not rude. This simply means not being aggressive or offensive to others.

Does not insist on its own way. This quality in a person means that she does not insist on her own rights. Human rights are important. But sometimes people forget that one person's right is apt to curtail the rights of others.

Not irritable. One possessing this quality does not take note of slights or hold grudges.

Not resentful. This is a bookkeeping term, meaning to keep account of debts with the purpose of squaring them later on. The concern here is that one not keep a record of evil done to her.

Does not rejoice in wrongdoing. This involves not finding pleasure in the wrong done by one person to another.

But rejoices in the truth. Another translation (NIV) of this phrase is "rejoices with the truth." Love is brave enough to face the truth and consistent enough to stand on the side of right.

Bears all things. This is not a passively enduring spirit, but a conquering spirit that rises above affliction.

Believes all things. This does not mean that one is gullible. Instead, she has the desire to put the best construction on what she hears or sees in others. It is the opposite of the spirit that constantly looks for wrong motives in others.

Hopes all things. A person who possesses this quality keeps on hoping on behalf of others even when hope has been repeatedly disappointed. Notice that both believing and hoping do not rule out a clear-eyed understanding of reality. This is not blind hope or belief. Rather it is the hope of love that what is best in the other person will eventually come to the fore. Such hope and belief have borne fruit in many lives.

Endures all things. This involves remaining true in the most adverse circumstances. (We should be careful here and note that this admonition from Paul is not intended to encourage Christians to remain in abusive relationships.)

Paul wrote his "poem to love" in the midst of a long lecture on the gifts of the Spirit (1 Cor. 12–14). In 1 Corinthians 13:8 he said that all these other gifts were only temporal and temporary. In the fullness of eternity, they will be unnecessary and will disappear. But love, because it is of the essence of God, will never end.

The Totality of Love

The truths of all these passages blend into and supplement one another. The Source of love, God, does not remain aloof from us. God dwells within us in the power of the Holy Spirit, changing us into the image of Jesus Christ. Thus the qualities of love are being created in us. These are elements of strength, signs of inward "all rightness" that make it possible to relate redemptively to others.

The *experience* of love comes to us through Jesus Christ. He has His permanent residence in the heart of each of His followers. He also lives in His church as He did in His body here on earth. He is vitally connected to the Source of love, so that He can bring the strength of God's love to bear fully on each life. He embodies all the attributes of love. We therefore have the true example of what it is like to love.

The *power* of love becomes ours through the Holy Spirit. This part of the Trinity makes actual in our lives what we see in the life of Jesus Christ and transmits to us the love that God has had for us from all eternity and for all eternity.

---

[1]William Owen Carver, *The Glory of God in the Christian Calling* (Nashville: Broadman Press, 1949), 138.

Questions for Thought and Discussion

1. What is your understanding of "God is love"? How has your understanding changed during the years?

2. Describe what God's love means to you.

3. Try to imagine what the love of Jesus Christ is like, as described in the prayer in Ephesians 3:18–19. Express your understanding in whatever medium is natural to you: writing it out, creating a poem, writing a simple chorus or hymn, drawing or painting your conception.

4. Describe Jesus in the terms of 1 Corinthians 13:4–7.

5. Examine your own attitude of love in relationship to the love of Christ.

Personal Action Plans

Acknowledging God the heavenly Parent as the Source of love, I will respond to this love in a new way this week by

Recognizing God the Son as the Experience of love, I will share this experience with someone this week by

Affirming God the Holy Spirit as the Power of love, I will become a conduit for this love this week by

11

Growing in Joy and Peace

While the previous chapter and this one lead us to consider specifically the "fruit of the Spirit" (Gal. 5:22–23), all of the elements of spiritual growth are fruit of the Spirit. Without the Spirit's inner working, we would not grow spiritually. But Paul set out a beautiful list of fruit—qualities—that God's Spirit produces in the Christian's life: "love, joy, peace, patience, kindness, generosity, faithfulness, gentleness, self-control." (Earlier chapters have covered several of these qualities.) These qualities do not happen automatically in our lives. They are the result of the combined work of the Spirit and of the individual Christian.

My backyard has many of the aspects of an orchard, with both peach and plum trees. I love everything about growing fruit. If I lived in a different climate, I might have several more varieties of trees. But I have learned to stick with the fruit that I can reasonably grow in a hot, semiarid climate like north central Texas. In the early spring the trees look like brides decked out in pink and white blossoms. I have almost nothing to do with this flowering. It depends on soil and moisture and the warmth of the sun.

But as soon as the petals begin to drop, my work begins. I have learned that three things are necessary on

98

my part for me to harvest fruit from my trees: consistent spraying for insects; supplemental watering; and thinning out the smaller fruits in order to have fewer, larger ones. If I do all these things faithfully, and if we have good weather conditions, my trees are laden with plums and peaches for several months.

Apply this example to the fruit of the Spirit. The Spirit provides the spark of life and the nutrients of spiritual growth. But we must provide discipline, care, obedience, and communion with God. Together these elements produce the fruit of the Spirit.

Love, joy, and peace are listed first in these spiritual qualities. This is no accident. The last chapter noted that love is the basis and the crown of spiritual growth. Love, joy, and peace express attitudes by which to face life. Our present chapter focuses on the way joy and peace can foster spiritual growth in the midst of life's negative aspects. As with love, joy and peace are both the fruit of spiritual growth and the basis for future growth.

Joy and Peace Displacing Anxiety

Romans 15:13; Philippians 4:4–7
Paul expressed his desire in Romans 15:13 (NRSV) that his readers might be filled "with all joy and peace in believing, so that you may abound in hope by the power of the Holy Spirit." He seemed to be saying that the Christian's trust in the "God of hope" would issue in joy and peace that would produce abundant hope for the future.

People who are not hopeful about the future are generally nagged by anxiety. If they do not believe that some good may lie ahead, they are plagued by uncertainty. That leads to worry and anxiety.

Paul expanded this idea in Philippians 4:4–7. As you read these words, remember that Paul was writing them from a Roman prison. If anyone had cause to worry, it was Paul. He had been in prison two years in Palestine, falsely accused by the Jews. Now he was in a prison in Rome, with no idea how long it might be before his case came before the emperor. (Acts closes with the statement that Paul spent at least two years under guard.) Nor could Paul predict the outcome of his trial. Who wouldn't worry about the future? But Paul had an antidote for worry and offered it to his friends in Philippi. "Rejoice in the Lord always," he said. Then, to be sure they understood him clearly, he said, "Again I will say, Rejoice" (NRSV).

Notice that this rejoicing was to be "in the Lord"—in their relationship with Jesus Christ, in what Jesus had promised that God would do for the children of God in the future. Rejoicing would lead to other results: The Christian would be forbearing. We might sum it up in the word *courtesy*. A courteous person is not always putting her own demands forward. The person who rejoices in her relationship with God through Christ is not always seeking to enhance herself at the expense of others. She can step aside and let someone else get in line.

Paul offered another reason for forbearance: "The Lord is near." The early church lived in constant expectation of Christ's quick return. While 2,000 years have blunted that expectation among us, Christ's return is far nearer now than it was in the first century. The person who rejoices in Christ and looks for His return will not be greatly concerned about getting what is "due" her in this life. She can be forbearing.

This kind of joy and faith in Christ calms anxiety (v. 6). Instead of fussing and stewing about the future, the Christian gives her future and her concerns about it to God in prayer. In this verse "prayer" refers to a general attitude of being in communion with God. "Supplication" refers to the specific petitions one brings to God in prayer. "Thanksgiving" is the expression of gratitude for blessings in the past. This remembrance is a reminder of God's faithfulness in caring for God's children. It engenders faith that God will continue to bless. Such praying leaves no room for anxiety about the future!

The attitude of forbearance and the practice of prayer blossom into peace in the heart of the believer (v. 7). This is the "peace of God"—the peace God gives. Such peace is beyond human understanding. It is the kind of peace that arouses amazement and even awe in those who do not possess it. "How can she be so serene?" they ask regarding the Christian who can face an uncertain future unafraid. The secret is in God, Who provides the peace.

The word *guard* had special meaning to the Philippians. It literally means to "act as a sentry," to "be a garrison." Philippi contained a military garrison. A garrison was an outpost of military personnel based in a city designated a Roman colony. The city had the status of a city of Rome, with all its privileges. Garrisons were generally located near the borders of the empire. Their purpose was to provide protection against the hordes of possible invaders from the barbarian tribes beyond the reach of the Roman government.

To speak of God's peace as being a garrison, therefore, meant that it would guard the Christian's most vulnerable parts from harm. The fear of the future might be compared to Roman fears of the invaders. No one knew when or if they might strike, but the potential was there. Still, Roman citizens, even on the borders, could sleep safely at night. They knew that the constant vigilance of the military garrisons would keep them from harm. This is an apt picture of the way God's peace protects each child of God. There is no need for anxiety when God is near.

Joy Transcending Suffering

Hebrews 12:2; James 1:2

Study these two verses side by side. James 1:2 (NRSV) states the principle: "Whenever you face trials of any kind, consider it nothing but joy." Hebrews 12:2 points to Jesus as the ultimate example of meeting suffering with joy. Paul is also an example to us. The keynote of his Philippian letter is joy.

How and why should Christians meet trials with joy? Notice, first, that these are trials, not temptations. Certainly no one should rejoice in temptations. But trials come because we belong to God. We are God's representatives in a world that is opposed to the divine will. Jesus warned His disciples that they would be persecuted by "the world." Yet in the face of this opposition He told His followers that they would have joy. As they followed Jesus' commands, especially to love one another, they would face opposition that would bring trials. But Jesus assured them that His joy would be in them and that their joy would be complete (John 15:10–11).

Jesus exemplified this attitude totally in the way He faced the Cross. Hebrews 12:2 tells us that He looked beyond the Cross to the joy He expected to find on the other side of it. This is the way to endure suffering. Those who can look beyond it can rejoice. A woman giving birth to a child looks beyond her immediate suffering to its result—a new life born into the world through her pain. This is the creative attitude toward suffering.

If we suffer because we are doing God's work in the world, we can be assured of victory in the end. In the light of that victory, we, like Jesus, can rejoice in our suffering because it contributes to the fulfillment of God's kingdom. Much of Jesus' joy was realized when He had "taken his seat at the right hand of the throne of God" (NRSV). He was then beginning to see the fruit of His suffering. This joy will continue throughout all time as people come to a redeemed relationship with God through Jesus' sacrifice.

Peace Growing Out of Discipline

Hebrews 12:11–14; James 3:17–18

These words from Hebrews 12 sound strange to modern ears. Discipline seems to be a lost emphasis. It even has an ugly sound. So what are we to make of these verses that speak so clearly of God's discipline?

First, we need to recognize that God does indeed discipline us, but not by coming down on us in anger. Actually, often God's discipline comes through the consequences of our waywardness. The person who uses drugs or overindulges in food, alcoholic drinks, or tobacco may not feel the "rod of the Lord" directly. But her body will feel the result of such abuse. This is only one example of the way God allows us to be disciplined.

I have experienced another way. Occasionally I have known I was taking a course or making a decision that God did not approve. At such times I have not felt the lack of God's presence. Rather, I have felt God very much present, grieving over what I was doing. I could sense God's silent urging to return to the way of righteousness. I can testify that such discipline had more to do with my change of attitude than any harsh punishment could have had.

God's discipline "yields the peaceful fruit of righteousness" (NRSV). Notice how these words are put together. "Peace" in Hebrew thought did not mean simply the absence of conflict. It was strongly positive. It referred, first, to everything that made for people's welfare. It referred, second, to right relationships between people. Righteousness and peace, therefore, belong together. A peace that is built on falsehood or the least common denominator is not true peace. The writer of Hebrews coupled peace and holiness in verse 14. Those who work for right relationships between people will work for peace. And true peace will be based on right relationships.

Discipline calls for people to make efforts toward right relationships between persons (peace) and toward holiness. Holiness means obedience to God and dedication to doing God's will. These efforts require strong actions. Verses 12–13 indicate the kind of actions people under discipline need to take.

James 3:17–18 looks at peace and righteousness from the perspective of wisdom. Chapter 3 in this book reminds us that wisdom means the understanding of spiritual truth. It can be summed up in the phrase, "the mind of Christ." Jesus' mind was set on obedience to God. Through His obedience He gained the wisdom to live as the Redeemer of all people.

James described wisdom by its characteristics. First, it is "pure." This may be called the inner characteristic of wisdom. It desires to cleanse the mind of all the elements that would cloud it and keep it from receiving spiritual truth. As the mind is continually undergoing this process, outward characteristics of wisdom appear. James outlined them for his readers.

There is being "peaceable"—the desire to maintain right relationships between people. "Gentle, willing to yield" refers to the ways people keep peace in relationships. The gentle person is forbearing, not always insisting on her own rights. The one who is willing to yield can be counted on to be reasonable, to follow orders for the good of all. This word in the Greek originally referred to children or slaves who had to obey those above them. That application would not fit here. But the flavor of the word is enduring. All of us are under God's will. Wisdom causes us to be readily obedient to that will.

"Mercy and good fruits" are linked together. Mercy is the attitude that issues in good deeds toward others. All of these qualities of wisdom are connected to being peaceable. Certainly, the person who puts these qualities to work in her relationships with others will reap good fruits, enduring relationships that issue in peace.

"Without a trace of partiality or hypocrisy" reflects purity. The one who keeps her mind free of impurities will not be uncertain or insincere. Her mind will be clear on the issues, and she will know how to act on them.

James concluded his teaching with an illustration from the harvest, similar to our earlier discussion of fruit. A harvest depends on the sowing. Those who desire peace will sow peace and will work for it. The harvest will be right relationships—which is peace.

The attitude of peace is not passive. It grows out of discipline. It is the determination to exert every effort to obey God and to establish right relationships with others. It is the necessary attitude for living as a child of God in this world.

Questions for Thought and Discussion

1. Recall a time in your life when you were uncertain of the future and worried about the outcome. What means did you use to return to a settled state of mind?

2. If you did not list joy as one of those means, consider how the "joy of the Lord" would have helped you in your time of anxiety. Write out your thoughts or share them with a friend.

3. If peace is the gift of God, why do we have to work for it?

4. What part do you think individual Christians can play in peace among people? In peace throughout the world? Give reasons for your answers.

Personal Action Plans

Acknowledging God's desire that I displace anxiety in my life with joy and peace, I give up my anxiety about _____________ and trust God, Who provides the peace.

Recognizing that I will face trials because I belong to God, I commit to meeting them with joy and will express that joy by

Affirming the need for God's discipline in my life, I will encourage God's loving discipline by

12

The Goal of Christian Growth

This chapter marks the end of our study of spiritual growth. And yet, the end is also the beginning! For the goal of spiritual growth is what God intended for us from the beginning of creation.

Chapter 1 reminded us that the chief goal of a Christian is "to glorify God and enjoy him forever." Glory means the outer showing forth of an inner quality or nature. An artist's painting is the artist's glory. It shows the genius hidden within her or him. A person's deeds of kindness are the glory of that individual. They show the spirit of love in her or his heart. So God's glory is seen through God's children. Those who are made in God's image should show the likeness of God in their lives.

But this does not happen automatically in our lives. A dog born of two Labrador retrievers will grow up to exhibit the characteristics of a Labrador. This is not true of human beings. We use the very characteristic that makes us most like God—free will—to rebel against God. So it is necessary for God to redeem His own creation: to bring us back into parent-child relationship. God did this through the life, death, and resurrection of Jesus Christ.

As we follow Jesus in faith, we become closely related to Him, so that there is a "family likeness." The purpose of this transformation is that Jesus "might be the first-born within a large family" (Rom. 8:29 NRSV). I see the aim of spiritual growth as being threefold: (1) to become increasingly Christlike in this life; (2) to attain a resurrected body like Christ's when we die; (3) to participate in the redemption of the whole created order. The Bible passages in this chapter relate to this aim. Many Bible verses deal with these matters. You might like to spend some time searching the New Testament to find references to the glory of the children of God. The passages this chapter highlights are, however, some of the most detailed teachings.

The Goal of Christlikeness

Ephesians 3:21; 4:13–16; 5:29–30; Colossians 1:18
Note primarily Ephesians 4:13–16. Then allow the other three passages to shed light on these verses. It is important to recognize that the goal of mature personhood (Eph. 4:13) belongs to the church, not to any individual Christian. All the pronouns referring to Christians in these verses are plural. Also, "the whole body" (v. 16) always means the church. Now read Colossians 1:18.

What is the purpose of the church? It is the same as that of Christ: to bring glory to God (Eph. 3:21).

If Christ is the head and the church is the body, there is just one organism. It is this total organism that is to bring glory to God. But just as the head receives more attention and honor than the body, so Christ has more honor. On the other hand, the head needs a body through which to function. In this world Christ needs the church through which to bring honor to His Father.

Ephesians 5:29–30 (NRSV) contains a similar thought. Paul had been comparing the church to the wife in a marital relationship. He said explicitly that Christ loves "the church, because we are members of his body." Christ loves the church because it is His own body expressing His likeness in the world.

How does the church show Christ's glory? What is the church's aim in showing Christ to the world? This is the theme of Ephesians 4:13–16. Paul called for "the unity of the faith and of the knowledge of the Son of God" (v. 13 NRSV). "Unity" here does not refer to organizational or organic union in the church. Rather, it refers back to verses 4–7: the beliefs that bind us to Christ and therefore to one another. The more we grow in our knowledge of Jesus Christ, the closer we come to Him and to one another. This oneness is essential if we are to show the world the glory of God. No body whose members bicker among themselves is able to function as one.

Paul then stated the ideal: that "all of us come . . . to maturity, to the measure of the full stature of Christ" (NRSV). This verse says a mouthful! It means that the whole church—all the Christians on the planet considered collectively—will display the glory of God as if Jesus Christ Himself were here.

What a tremendous idea! Certainly no one person, no one group, could do such a thing adequately. Within ourselves, within our own small church groups, we can see too many of our faults and failures. It takes all Christians, witnessing, serving, loving, suffering, to exemplify the life of Jesus in the world. It still is an ideal we have not attained. Paul set it up as a standard toward which to strive.

In the next three verses (Eph. 4:14–16) Paul gave some ideas as to how we can attain such maturity of spiritual life. He began with the negative, in verse 14. This verse is filled with word pictures and vivid similes. Perhaps a paraphrase will make it clearer. W. O. Carver, in his book on Ephesians, *The Glory of God in the Christian Calling*, interpreted the verse in this way. (In order to get a clear understanding, read this paraphrase through completely, without pausing at the parentheses):

"In order that we may be no longer babes, (no longer) carried about on tossing waves and blown hither and yon by every wind of doctrine (that may come along, teaching no more stable and reliable than one may see) in the dice throw of the (mere gambling) men, or (as subject to what event may show up) in the sleight of hand (performance) that promotes the cunning of deceit (on the part of exploiters)."[1]

The parentheses were inserted to show where Carver interpreted the meaning of words, rather than simply translating them. But the message is clear: Instability, gullibility, and trickery are all traits of the immature personality.

Paul then turned to the positive aspect of his teaching with verses 15–16. He pointed out the importance of "speaking the truth in love." Carver said that Paul put in this point because we are all members of the same body. How tragic it would be for different members of the same body to put on masks of piety, flattery, or pretense toward one another. So, Carver said, it is important to put aside falsehood and accept the principle of oneness in the body.

Having established this principle, the members of the body then may "grow up in every way into him who is the head, into Christ." This statement does not mean that all members become the head. They grow up in the way that the head determines.

Verse 16 is a delightful reflection of medical knowledge in Paul's day. (I sometimes wonder whether he got his information from "the beloved physician," Luke.) The main point is that the healthy body is in tune with its head and with itself. As members determine to follow the head, they grow under his leadership and in harmony with one another. And the energy that powers such growth is love—*agape* love.

Will this ideal be fulfilled in this world? Probably not. For even the entire church to mirror perfectly the character of Christ seems impossible. But the clearest picture of our Savior will be seen in His church. This picture is only a foretaste of what is to come.

The Goal of the Resurrected Body

1 John 3:2; Philippians 3:21; 1 Corinthians 15:45–50
The second goal of spiritual growth is to have a resurrected body like that of Christ. You may wonder how this relates to the goal of Christlikeness. Is the Resurrection body not something that God will give us at the end of time? What does our spiritual growth have to do with that?

Review the truths of 1 John 3:1–3 (see chap. 2). Verse 2 promises that, when we will see Jesus, we will be like Him. That is the promise of the Resurrection body. But the next verse says that those with such a hope continue to purify themselves. They grow more and more to be like the one whose likeness they hope to bear.

In a way that we do not comprehend, our spiritual growth is related to the body we will have in the Resurrection. God will certainly make up for our deficiencies of character when we are given new bodies. But God expects us to work now toward becoming the persons we will be throughout eternity. Eternal life begins with our profession of faith in Jesus Christ. What we do with our lives now has eternal significance. The more we grow toward Christlikeness, the more we are preparing ourselves for the lives we will be living when we see Him "face to face."

Remember that when Jesus appeared to His disciples after His resurrection, He was not a stranger to them. They did not always recognize him immediately. But when He "revealed" Himself to them, He was the familiar Master they had known before His death.

Paul explained some of the mystery about the Resurrection body in 1 Corinthians 15:40–45. But our best understanding really comes from knowing that we will (1) still be who we are; and (2) have a body fitted for a new life, just like the one Jesus has (Phil. 3:21).

With these ideas in mind, look at 1 Corinthians 15:40–45. In this passage Paul was pointing out all the various forms of life with which he and his readers were familiar. "Glory" in these verses again means the showing forth of an inner nature. Each form of life has a body that expresses its functions and nature in the created order.

Then Paul compared the physical body with the spiritual body. As the physical body is designed to live in this temporal world, the spiritual body will be fitted to live in the eternal world. Paul made several comparisons to show the difference between the body of earth and the body of eternity. What is sown (buried after death) is perishable. Our bodies are not constructed to last forever. Throughout our lifetimes there is movement toward death.

What is sown is also in dishonor. God did not intend for us to live in a state of corruption and sinfulness. God said of creation, including humanity, that it was "very good." We have certainly not turned out that way! Rather than living in glory, showing forth the image of the Creator, human beings have been far less than God intended. So humanity has lived in dishonor. But God's children will be raised in glory! Finally we will show forth the image of God as we were created to do.

Also, the sowing is in weakness. In spite of human beings' superior brainpower, our bodies are essentially weak. Scientists are constantly fighting the threats of disease and death. It takes so little to kill a human being! But the spiritual body will be characterized by power. The children of God will move at will throughout the universe. They will have in their bodies the power that Jesus demonstrated when He was raised from the dead and when He ascended into heaven. Our redeemed bodies will be a new kind of self that is perfectly adapted to life under the leadership of the Holy Spirit.

The Goal: Redeemed Creation

Romans 8:18–21

This goal completes the whole cycle of redemption. A redeemed personality demands a spiritual body through which to function. And a spiritual body requires a redeemed environment in which to live. Furthermore, God never intended for creation, which He pronounced very good, to be totally lost. God does not create for futility!

The Bible is rather quiet on this topic. Our verses from Romans 8 embody perhaps one of the most elaborate statements about the redeemed creation. Verse 18 links the redemption of the created order with the glory of the children of God. Verses 19–21 speak from the viewpoint of creation, which eagerly longs "for the revealing of the children of God" (NRSV). At the end of time all creation will be redeemed from its bondage to decay. This bondage is the never-ending cycle of birth and death, growth and decline, creating and destroying that is integral to nature as we now know it.

But this will not always be so. God's plans for creation are good, as they always have been. Everything will come in its season. Now is the time for the cycle of life and death. In the future will come the time for the redeemed creation to blossom—and never fade away.

---

[1]William Owen Carver, *The Glory of God in the Christian Calling* (Nashville: Broadman Press, 1949), 151.

Questions for Thought and Discussion

(These questions are designed as a review of the whole book.)

1. What does the title of this book, *Until Christ Is Formed in You,* mean to you now?

2. Consider the elements of spiritual growth as summarized in "Linking the Elements" at the end of chapter 4. How do you see these as being helpful in your growth in the future?

3. Look at the areas of spiritual growth. Which ones are being exemplified in your life? Where would you like to see more growth?

4. Think of the goal of spiritual growth. Write out in your own words what these parts of the goal mean to you. How do they increase your joy in being a Christian?

Personal Action Plans

Recognizing that Christ uses the church to bring honor to God, I will do my part through my church by

Acknowledging that what I do with my life now affects the person I will be in eternity, I will grow toward Christ-likeness by

About the writer
Velma Darbo Stevens has been involved in writing Bible studies all of her adult life. A graduate of the Southern Baptist Theological Seminary in Louisville, Kentucky, she was for nearly 20 years an editor of Bible study materials at the Baptist Sunday School Board (now LifeWay Christian Resources). An author of five other books, she currently does freelance writing and editing of religious materials. Velma is an active member of Broadway Baptist Church in Fort Worth, Texas, where she writes weekly Bible study helps for adult teachers.